"BUT I DO CLAMOR"

MAY WRIGHT SEWALL

A LIFE, 1844–1920

Ray E. Boomhower

Guild Press of Indiana
Zionsville, Indiana

For Megan, who made all my dreams come true.

Other books by Ray E. Boomhower

Jacob P. Dunn, Jr.: A Life in History and Politics, 1855–1924
The Country Contributor: The Life and Times of Juliet Strauss
Destination Indiana: Travels through Hoosier History

"What office is there which involves more responsibility, which requires more qualifications, and which ought, therefore, to be more honourable, than that of teaching?"

Harriet Martineau (1802–1876), English writer

Contents

Preface

To commemorate the end of the twentieth century, the *Indianapolis Star* in December 1999 announced its "10 Greatest Hoosiers of the 20th Century." The century's greatest figures for the nineteenth state had been voted on by 6,753 newspaper readers, who cast their votes in what the *Star* claimed was "one of the largest reader participation projects in the newspaper's history." Readers could pick from a ballot in the newspaper listing sixty-five Hoosiers, or write in their favorites. When the votes were counted, those receiving the most ballots were (in order): businessman Eli Lilly, poet James Whitcomb Riley, journalist Ernie Pyle, composer Cole Porter, astronaut Virgil "Gus" Grissom, songwriter Hoagy Carmichael, comedian Red Skelton, businesswoman Madam C. J. Walker, basketball star Larry Bird, and former Indianapolis Motor Speedway owner Tony Hulman.[1]

Of course, anyone with an interest in the state's history could argue for the inclusion of other names to this select list of Hoosier legends. As someone who in the past wrote on the life and tragic death of Grissom, I was pleased to see the Mitchell, Indiana, native in the top ten, and happily discussed the astronaut's impact on the state with *Star* columnist Nelson Price for his articles on the greatest Hoosiers. The whole idea soon passed from my mind after the media frenzy on the millennium faded.

I began to rethink the subject, however, after a telephone conversation with Nancy Baxter of Guild Press of Indiana. In that conversation we discussed possible subjects for Guild Press's series, Indiana Women Who Made a Difference, which I had helped inaugurate in 1998 with my biography of "The County Contributor," Juliet Strauss of Rockville, Indiana. The name that immediately sprang to my mind for the series was a woman who had an impact not only on life in Indiana but also on the nation and the world as well: teacher, suffragette, and peace activist May Wright Sewall. As someone who deals every day in Indiana history,

I knew something about Sewall and her career. In spite of her accomplishments, I was not surprised that she failed to crack the *Star*'s top ten list. But after talking with Price, who organized the project for the newspaper, I learned that Sewall did garner enough votes from readers (398) to finish forty-fourth in the balloting, ranking a slot above Indiana Pacers star Reggie Miller, but below Indiana University sex researcher Alfred Kinsey.

What writer could resist immersing himself in the life of a woman who worked with such national suffrage leaders as Susan B. Anthony and Elizabeth Cady Stanton; endeavored to improve Indianapolis's cultural landscape by being an active founder of such groups as the Indianapolis Woman's Club, the Propylaeum, Contemporary Club, and Art Association of Indianapolis; campaigned for peace with Henry Ford and others on the automobile magnate's ill-fated trip to Europe during the early days of World War I; and explored what may lie beyond the grave through spiritualism? It was a life filled with triumphs and tragedies, and one well worth retelling to a new generation. I am proud that this effort marks the third volume in Guild Press' Indiana Women Who Made a Difference series.

My interest in Sewall peaked considerably early in my research when I discovered a letter to her from author Elbert Hubbard, a frequent visitor to the suffragist's home in Indianapolis. Writing his friend following an 1897 lecture in the capital city, Hubbard related that on the way to the railroad station he chanced to meet a "strange man" who told him that he had attended Hubbard's talk. The man, wrote Hubbard, made "slighting and slurring" remarks about Jacob Piatt Dunn Jr., a noted Indiana historian and journalist on whom I wrote a biography in 1997. Dunn, the man claimed, did not possess "the gold of silence," and went on to note about the lecture: "But didn't Mrs. Sewall apply the snuffers to him gracefully—oh that was good!" Anyone who could best Dunn in conversation is worthy of respect.[2]

The life of a person researching and writing a biography is not a lonely one. A biographer makes the journey into the past accompanied by many people, including scholars who have come before him. I am particularly indebted to Indianapolis author Hester Anne Hale, who generously granted me permission to cite material from her unpublished work, "May Wright Sewall: Avowed Feminist," a copy of which is maintained in the Indiana Historical Society's William Henry Smith Memorial Library.

Lending invaluable assistance and advice on the manuscript were two fine editors, Paula Corpuz, IHS senior editor, and Megan McKee, freelance editor (who also happens to be my wife). Both Paula and Megan gave up their personal time to lend their editorial skills to the book. Of course, any errors or omissions in the book are mine and mine alone.

I would also like to thank Catherine Gibson, former manager, adult services, at the Indianapolis–Marion County Public Library, for granting me access to Sewall's papers and for urging me to write about Sewall's life "warts and all." As always, offering invaluable assistance were the staffs at the IHS Library, the Indiana State Library's Indiana Division, and Lilly Library at Indiana University. Without their help this book, and many others, could never be written.

I also must express a debt of gratitude to my in-laws, Ann and Roy McKee of New Castle, who offered me a quiet place to work while I put in long hours on this manuscript during weekends.

Again last, but never least, my heartfelt thanks to Nancy Baxter at Guild Press of Indiana for publishing the book and for her continued support of Indiana women's history.

Chronology

1844	Born in Milwaukee County, Wisconsin, to Philander Montague and Mary Weeks (Brackett) Wright (27 May)
1866	Receives mistress of science degree from Northwestern Female College
1872	Marries Edwin W Thompson (2 March)
1873	Edwin Thompson serves as superintendent of Franklin schools, May as principal of high school
1874	The Thompsons accept teaching jobs at Indianapolis High School
1875	Edwin W. Thompson dies of tuberculosis in South Carolina (August 19) May Thompson helps found Indianapolis Woman's Club
1878	May Thompson and others organize the Indianapolis Equal Suffrage Society
1880	May Thompson marries Theodore Lovett Sewall (30 October)
1882	The Sewalls establish the Girls' Classical School in Indianapolis
1883	Art Association of Indianapolis organized (7 May)

1888	International Council of Women meeting held in Washington, D.C. (25 March to 1 April)
	Indianapolis Propylaeum incorporated (6 June)
1890	Contemporary Club holds its first meeting (25 September)
1891	Dedication ceremonies for Propylaeum building on North Street (27 January)
1893	World's Congress of Representative Women meeting held at World Exposition in Chicago (15 May)
1894	May Wright Sewall selected as president of International Council of Women at meeting in London
1895	May Wright Sewall receives news of John Herron bequest for Art Association (13 May)
	Theodore Sewall dies of tuberculosis (23 December)
1902	Art Association occupies the former Talbott property and opens the John Herron Art Institute (11 February)
1905	May Wright Sewall enters into a partnership with Anna F. Weaver for operating the Girls' Classical School
1907	Sewall announces her retirement from management of the Girls' Classical School (February)

1915   Sewall organizes International Conference of Women Workers to Promote International Peace in San Francisco (July)

Henry Ford asks Sewall to serve as a delegate on his peace trip to Europe aboard the *Oscar II*; ship sets sail for Europe on 4 December

1919   Sewall returns to Indianapolis to live

1920   Bobbs-Merrill publishes Sewall's book on her spiritualist experiences, *Neither Dead nor Sleeping*

Sewall dies in Indianapolis (22 July)

Prologue

While preparing for classes one day on the third floor at Indianapolis High School (later to become Shortridge), a teacher who had come to the city with her husband in the 1870s was interrupted by a distinguished visitor: Zeralda Wallace, widow of Governor David Wallace and president of the Woman's Christian Temperance Union's Indiana chapter. Wallace had come to the school to ask the teacher, May Wright Sewall, to sign a petition in favor of temperance Wallace planned on presenting to the state legislature. Sewall was preparing to add her name to the document when her eye caught some words indicating that those who signed did not intend to "clamor" for any additional civil or political rights. "But I do clamor," Sewall exclaimed to Wallace. Throwing the paper on the floor, Sewall stalked out of the room, "vexed in soul that I had been dragged down three flights of stairs to see one more proof of the degree to which honorable women love to humiliate themselves before men for sweet favor's sake."[1]

Sewall's anger at Wallace faded over time, and the two joined forces to found the Indianapolis Equal Suffrage Society. The society came about in large part due to the "open contempt" showed to Wallace by Hoosier legislators when she attempted to present her temperance petition to the Indiana General Assembly. One lawmaker even went so far as to tell Wallace that since women held no political power, her document "might as well have been signed by 10,000 mice."[2] To ensure that women's voices would indeed be heard by those in power, Sewall worked tirelessly on behalf of rights for women in the United States—and around the world—during the late nineteenth and early twentieth centuries. She served as an invaluable ally to such national suffrage leaders as Susan B. Anthony and

Elizabeth Cady Stanton, and gave the woman's movement an international focus through her pioneering involvement with the International Council of Women and the American National Council of Women. Through these groups, a Sewall biographer noted, she hoped to "unite for common purposes representatives of women's organizations of all types, at home and abroad—professional, educational, cultural, religious, welfare, and reform."[3] By the turn of the twentieth century, *Harper's Bazaar* magazine claimed that Sewall had "an 'eternal feminine' following of 5,000,000 in eleven countries." Her stature internationally was such that even royalty was impressed. During a garden party hosted by Britain's Queen Victoria during an International Council of Women meeting, a London newspaper reported that notwithstanding the numerous titled women present at the occasion, Sewall was "the only one who made the court bow as if she were used to it."[4]

Her involvement in the suffrage movement was but one part of Sewall's extensive participation in a number of activities that covered, as fellow Hoosier suffragist Ida Husted Harper noted, "a broader field than those of most women and in all of these she was by nature and ability a leader."[5] Born in Wisconsin to a family that encouraged its precocious daughter's thirst for betterment through education, Sewall and her "powerful, dominant and queenly personality" became a familiar sight on Indianapolis's streets, where she had moved in 1874 with her first husband, Edwin W. Thompson (who died a year later from tuberculosis), after a teaching stint in the Franklin school system.[6] She quickly won for herself the devotion of her Indianapolis students. A local newspaper even claimed that she was "more talked of in the homes of the city by the young persons who met her in class work than all the other members of the faculty. The thing called personal magnetism or 'personality' . . . quickly impressed itself upon all who met her, either old or young, and she never lost that peculiar quality."[7] Although her friends and supporters considered Sewall as far and away Indiana's outstanding woman of the early twentieth century, there were others who frowned on her liberal ideas on such issues as higher education for women and equality of the sexes. Mary Mc-Laughlin, a Sewall neighbor, remembered coming upon the educator one day while walking down North Pennsylvania Street with her mother. "Like most well-known and prominent people in the school life and club life of our city," McLaughlin said of Sewall, "she was criticized very severely, for things she probably never did or said." The backbiting sometimes disturbed Sewall, who complained bitterly to McLaughlin's mother about being misunderstood by her fellow Indianapolis citizens.[8]

Sewall's commitment to equal rights for her sex occurred during a time when advocating the enfranchisement of women was looked on as laughable by some and dangerous by others. In 1878, when Sewall wished to bring together women with "advanced ideas" to discuss the possibility of forming an Indianapolis suffrage association, she had to do so through "a secretly circulated summons." The meeting, which drew nine women and one man, included a lengthy discussion on whether or not the new organization should take for itself a name that would hide from the public its primary purpose, or one boldly stating its intention. Looking back on the birth of the Indianapolis Equal Suffrage Society from the vantage point of eight years, Sewall marveled over the fact that "ten conscientious, upright persons could thus secretly convene in an obscure room, and that such a question could agitate them for more than two hours." The incident, she added, was the "best indication that could be given of the conservative atmosphere which enveloped Indianapolis."[9]

Sewall even had the temerity to propose a new word to express the same meaning for a friendship between women as the word fraternal did for men. In a speech before the Indianapolis Woman's Club in 1882, Sewall pointed out that for the word sister, Webster's Dictionary had derivatives with accompanying definitions and examples that occupied only twenty-nine lines, while sixty-eight lines were devoted to meanings and illustrations of the use of ten derivatives for the word brother. "The revelation," reported the *Indianapolis Times*'s "Our Town" columnist Anton Scherrer, "stunned the Woman's Club. So much so that time had to be called to allow the ladies to collect themselves." Once order had been restored, Sewall went on to suggest the word "sorosal" or "sororal" to indicate the sisterly regard women have for one another.[10]

Her work on behalf of suffrage for women was just one of the many reform and cultural endeavors Sewall became involved in during her life. Described by one Indianapolis acquaintance as "a large woman of sturdy carriage," Sewall played a significant role in the cultural and social life of the capital city. At first with her second husband, the Harvard-educated Theodore Lovett Sewall, and later alone, she operated the influential Girls' Classical School, located on the southeast corner of Pennsylvania and Saint Joseph Streets. The private school provided hundreds of young women with the rigorous mental and physical training they needed in order to further their education in such respected institutions of higher learning as Vassar, Smith, Wellesley, and Mount Holyoke. "There be those who, believing that sex enters the mind, assumes that therefore there must be feminine studies for feminine minds," said Sewall. "It would be just as logical to provide feminine foods for feminine bodies; but it is universally admitted that milk is good for babies of both sexes, and meat for the mature of both."[11] Sewall championed reform not only for what women were taught, but for what they wore as well, advocating a "simple school dress" that enabled her students to participate in physical fitness exercises, including daily gymnastics.[12] "We forgot Xenophon easily," said Charlotte Cathcart, one of her students, "but not Mrs. Sewall."[13]

Her students displayed a lifelong loyalty to their former mentor. When a report circulated in Indianapolis in 1902 that Sewall's school was going to be abandoned due to financial difficulties, a group of alumnae distributed a resolution to newspapers expressing its gratitude to Sewall and claiming that the school "has filled a useful and honorable place in this community, and the benefits it has conferred and will always confer, make it desirable that it should be one of the permanent institutions of the city."[14] Unfortunately, those wishes fell victim to the harsh dictates of financial difficulties, brought about from increased competition from public schools and other private institutions. Although Sewall attempted to forestall the inevitable by entering into a partnership with Anna F. Weaver in 1905, two years later Sewall announced her retirement and in 1910 Weaver closed the school for good.[15]

The Sewalls' residence, known as Sewall House, served as a cultural showcase for the city, hosting a variety of nationally known literary and political figures. Every Wednesday in the home's drawing room approximately one hundred to two hundred people of all types gathered to discuss the issues of the day. "This salon is distinctively the social and literary centre of all Indiana, and, for that matter, many a distinguished sojourner from antipodal parts had enjoyed this rare hospitality," noted *Harper's Bazaar*.[16] Another journalist who visited the house's library marveled over the fact that more "schemes for social progress have been conceived in this room . . . than in any other room on this continent."[17] A bold statement, but not surprising considering Sewall enriched the city's intellectual life through her efforts to form such organizations as the Indianapolis Woman's Club, the Art Association of Indianapolis (the forerunner of the Indianapolis Museum of Art), the Indianapolis Propylaeum, the Contemporary Club, the Ramabai Circle (a group working to aid women in India), the Alliance Francaise, and the Indiana branch of the Western Association of Collegiate Alumnae. In addition to all this, and her work at the school, she also found time to edit the woman's page in the Sunday edition of the *Indianapolis Times* from 1882 to 1885. No less an authority on life in Indianapolis than Booth Tarkington boldly claimed that in company with Benjamin Harrison and James Whitcomb Riley, Sewall "would necessarily have been chosen (in the event of a contest in such a matter) as one of the 'three most prominent citizens' of the place."[18]

The efforts made by Sewall to improve life for people were not merely parochial in nature, but international as well. In addition to lecturing widely across the United States on behalf of woman's rights, she also strove to win people's support for another cause: world peace, an effort she called her "absorbing ideal."[19] Although sometimes women had to fight to protect their homes and families, Sewall said that "no woman within civilization has ever been found who did not see in war . . . a menace to the whole spirit of the home, a menace to the children born and reared within the home; hence no woman within civilization who does not see war to be her constitutional and inevitably relentless foe." The only battle to which a woman could give her heart, she continued, "is that war whose object it is to slay war and establish peace."[20] Following the motto "My country is the world, my countrymen are all mankind," Sewall promoted the cause of peace through membership in the American Peace Society and through her work with both the National Council of Women and the International Council of Women, both of which adopted peace programs after intense lobbying by Sewall.

When war broke out in Europe in 1914 and many peace advocates believed their efforts had been for naught, Sewall persevered. To her, the conflict "seemed a proclamation to the women of the world that some action by them which would assert the solidarity of womanhood was imperative."[21] In 1915 Sewall organized and chaired an International Council of Women Workers to Promote Permanent Peace at the Panama-Pacific Exposition in San Francisco. To instill pacifism in young people, she called on textbook publishers to eliminate jingoistic language and to replace it with calls for brotherhood. She also implored mothers to remove toys that might "bring into a child's mind the thought of military pomp and show, of warfare, with its contentions and its glories."[22]

Her work for the peace movement came to a climax in November 1915 when automobile tycoon Henry Ford asked Sewall to join him and others interested in securing an end to the war that had engulfed Europe. "The people of the belligerent countries did not want the war," Ford wrote Sewall. "The people did not make it. The people want peace. It is their human right to get a chance to make it." He begged the Hoosier reformer to respond to this "call of humanity and join the consecrated spirits who have already signified a desire to help make history in a new way. The people of Europe cry out to you."[23] Sewall became one of sixty delegates to join Ford aboard the *Oscar II*, which sailed for Norway in hopes of getting the boys out of the trenches before Christmas. Most of the reporters onboard the ship—including Hoosier Elmer Davis, representing the *New York Times*—treated the expedition as a colossal joke. The newsmen organized an "Ancient and Honorable Order of the Vacillating Sons of St. Vitus," which had its headquarters at the ship's bar. Burnet Hershey, a young reporter on the voyage, claimed that the reporters pledged to "drink it [the bar] dry before they reached Norway."[24]

In a letter from the voyage addressed "To All My Friends in Hoosierdom," Sewall noted that the delegates' mission was to end the war and "rescue all the soldiers of all the armies from their present terrible situation by taking away their occupation," but they did not expect that the war would end simultaneously with their arrival in Europe. All the delegates hoped, and some expected, however, that their efforts might shorten the war, Sewall added. She added that the peace pilgrimage would accomplish the following:

> . . . arrest public attention, divert it from war to Peace, it will stimulate other private initiatives and encourage Peace workers in all lands, it will react on all of its participants to confirm the resolution of each to work for Permanent Peace until its condition shall have been secured. . . . Believe me! we are not hair-brained lunatics bent on a fool's errand—but rather a company of clear-headed but simple-hearted men and women, with no illusions in regard to ourselves but with the faith that *any one* of us, much more *all of us with* God, constitutes a majority in that council where each next step along the path of human progress is determined.[25]

The Ford expedition failed in its mission, and World War I dragged on until American intervention helped to turn the tide for the Allies. But Sewall's other numerous local, national, and international achievements won for her a well-deserved reputation for possessing "the 'organizing touch.'"[26] In a sketch of her work for the *Indianapolis Sentinel,* a reporter noted that Sewall had "a faculty for getting people to work together and setting them at work in useful lines—a sort of social clockmaker who gets human machinery into shape, winds it up and sets it to running."[27]

Her powerful personality, however, engendered not only loyalty but also loathing. She may have won the confidence of national suffrage leaders such as Anthony, but in Indiana Sewall engaged in a bitter and public battle for control of the Indiana National Woman Suffrage Association with Lafayette's Helen Gougar. Fellow Indiana suffragist Grace Julian Clarke described her friend Sewall as the "embodiment of intense vitality." Throughout most of Sewall's life, said Clarke, the reformer "hardly knew fatigue or the physical limitations that halt most of us in the prosecution of our endeavors." Although this characteristic aided the reformer in her varied causes, it did make her appear at times to be unfeeling. "She really could not understand, I think," Clarke noted, "that others grew weary when her own bodily mechanism functioned so perfectly." Sewall, however, never frightened Clarke, who always "felt quite free and unconstrained in her society, as I think most young persons did."[28]

Fellow suffragists viewed their colleague as "a preëminently common-sense woman." Unbeknownst to all but a handful of friends, however, Sewall led a secret life—one involving communicating with loved ones after their deaths. For nineteen years (four years of betrothal and an additional fifteen years of marriage) Sewall had enjoyed "happiness as perfect as humans may experience" through her relationship with Theodore Sewall, who had fully supported the reform causes she championed during her busy life. Those who knew the couple were impressed by their commitment to each other. Hoosier suffragist and Anthony biographer Ida Husted Harper called the marriage "one of the happiest and most perfrect homes ever made by two mortals."[29] A fortnight before his death from tuberculosis in 1895, Theodore told his wife that after dying the "first thing I shall do will be to ascertain whether or not Jesus ever returned to earth after His crucifixion." Once he uncovered this mystery he informed her that he would do "nothing else until I shall have succeeded in returning to you, unless before that time, you have come to me."[30]

Left "stunned and desolate" by her husband's death, Sewall attempted to forget her grief through work, especially her responsibilities at the Girls' Classical School and on behalf of world peace. Theodore Sewall remained in her thoughts, however, as she inscribed under large, framed photographs of the former educator in her home and at the school his creed: "To be well and to be at work is to have the two conditions necessary to happiness." She did work so hard that she forgot about Theodore Sewall's declaration about returning to her in some way. When two friends (one an officer in Sewall's Unitarian Church) approached her and beseeched her to visit a local medium so she might communicate with her departed mate, the proposal stunned Sewall. "It seemed to me grossly to violate both reason and delicacy," she said.[31]

Her journey into the spiritual world began two years after her husband's death while attending a Chautauqua meeting at a Spiritualist retreat located in Lily Dale, New York. Although she had been determined to leave the area immediately after speaking at the meeting, a series of unexplained accidents caused her to eventually meet with a "slate writer." Provided with a clean slate that never left her hands, Sewall, in turn, gave the medium a list of questions. Taking the slate back to her hotel room, the suffragist was astonished to find "perfectly coherent, intelligent and characteristic replies to questions which had been written upon the bits of paper that had not left my hands." This experience gave her "actual knowledge, if not of immortality, at least of a survival of death—I had learned that the last enemy is destroyed, in that he can destroy neither being nor identity, nor continuity of relationship."[32]

Until her death on 22 July 1920 Sewall claimed to be in almost constant contact with her dead husband, who told her to be very cautious in revealing her discovery to others as they would not believe her experiences of life after death. The few people to whom she related her fantastical adventures with the spiritual world—including former Indiana University president and biologist David Starr Jordan and philosopher William James—were unanimous in their belief that their friend was suffering from a mental delusion. In addition to her husband, Sewall communicated with other deceased relatives, received instruction on the piano from Anton Rubinstein, and received medical advice from Père Condé, a medieval priest and physician from France, which cured her Bright's disease.

The messages from beyond the grave often came in the form of "impressions" on her mind, which she then transcribed onto paper through a process called automatic writing. Sewall told a reporter for the *Indianapolis Star* that the communications from the dead came to her "as though one received a blow on the brain—not physically of course—but clear and distinct and without warning. And in an instant comes a complete train of thought—swift—immediate—not arrived at by the slow and ordinary sequence of ideas—a complete train of thought solving some heretofore unsolvable riddle of the universe."[33] She related her remarkable experiences with spiritualism in her book *Neither Dead nor Sleeping*, published by Bobbs-Merrill of Indianapolis in 1920 just a few months before Sewall's death.

Featuring a sympathetic introduction written by Tarkington, whose own sister Hauté dabbled in spiritualism, the spiritualist work "rocked the foundations of Indianapolis" and stunned those who knew the woman's rights crusader. "The book . . . took everybody by surprise," said *Indianapolis Times* columnist Scherrer, "because nobody around here had the least idea that Mrs. Sewall was in touch with the spirit world."[34] The suffragist related to an Indianapolis reporter that she undertook the work only because "extreme feebleness" had taken her permanently out of public affairs, giving her the necessary time to gather together the hundreds of record books she had on her spiritualist experiences.[35]

Although her former friends in Indianapolis were shocked by the revelations made in Sewall's book, spiritualism and woman's suffrage had enjoyed close ties ever since strange rappings from disembodied spirits disturbed the home of John and Margaret Fox in Hydesville, New York, in March 1848. When adherents of spiritualism gathered together, they welcomed woman's suffrage speakers and embraced the feminist movements' call for equal rights. The official *History of Woman Suffrage* edited by Stanton and Anthony claimed that Spiritualists were the only religious sect in the world to recognize the equality of women. "They have always assumed that woman may be a medium of communication from heaven to earth," the *History* noted, "that the spirits of the universe may breathe through her lips."[36] As Barbra Goldsmith observed in her biography of suffragist and spiritualist Victoria Woodhull, during a time when women held little or no power in either church or state affairs, they instead "relied on the 'other powers' provided by Spiritualism to sustain their efforts."[37]

Tarkington, who advised Sewall on her unique manuscript and helped to find a publisher for her work, considered three possible explanations for her possible communications with "'supernatural beings.'" One, she had over the past twenty years been laboring under a hallucination or a series of hallucinations. Two, Sewall's communications from the dead were really the work of her subconscious, the part of the mind, said Tarkington, that "constructs our dreams." The third and final possibility, the best-selling author said, was that the communications outlined by Sewall really were from "people we speak of as dead; but really they live." In considering these three theories, Tarkington concluded that the truth rested somewhere between the second and third. Whatever conclusion the reader reached about Sewall after perusing "this extraordinary book," said Tarkington, the one certain thing that shone forth was the writer's character. "And the one thing most vivid here is good will—the longing, in all humility, to be of great help to the world," he noted. "*That* explanation of Mrs. Sewall's book is undeniable."[38]

In spite of Tarkington's kind efforts on her behalf, Sewall and her work often received, at best, patronizing attention. But nothing, not even her dependence on a discredited belief system as a balm for her "intense grief, unutterable anguish" over the loss of her husband, can alter the breadth and depth of her accomplishments. Unbound by tradition, she endeavored to do all she could for causes still being fought for today—education, woman's rights, cultural enrichment, and world peace. The lasting legacies of her many works can still be seen in Indianapolis. The year 2000 marked the 125th anniversary of the Indianapolis Woman's Club, the Propylaeum remains as a place for women to gather and discuss the day's issues, and the Art Association of Indianapolis has grown into the internationally-respected Indianapolis Museum of Art. Sewall's friend and confidante Clarke offered the finest eulogy for Sewall and what she represented to women in Indiana, the United States, and the world when she said: "I never left Mrs. Sewall's presence without resolving to be more outspoken in good causes, more constant in their service, without a fresh resolve to let trivial concerns go and emphasize only really vital interests."[39]

Chapter 1

THE TEACHER

On 11 July 1848 in the *Seneca County Courier* a notice appeared stating that a two-day convention would be held at the Wesleyan Chapel in Seneca Falls, New York, beginning in seven days whose purpose was "to discuss the social, civil, and religious condition and rights of women." The first women's rights convention, organized by such pioneers in the struggle as Elizabeth Cady Stanton and Lucretia Mott, brought together 300 men and women to vote on a "Declaration of Sentiments" based on the Declaration of Independence and outlining "the repeated injuries and usurpations on the part of man towards woman." In addition to the declaration, the assembly barely passed a controversial resolution that it was "the duty of the women of the country to secure to themselves their sacred rights to the elective franchise," a right held at that time by no woman in the world. The resolution on woman's enfranchisement, helped in passage in no small part by the intercession of Frederick Douglass, eventually became the most important goal of woman's rights leaders. Early feminists, however, also sought changes in the legal, educational, and economic status of women.[1]

The women and men who gathered at Seneca Falls were the vanguard of a movement that sought to alter the way women were treated in the United States. In nineteenth-century American society, females were second-class citizens whose proper place consisted of being in the home serving the needs of their husbands and children. Although women in New York had been given the sole right to the property they owned before marriage in 1848, most women in the country did not have this privilege nor the legal custody of their children or the right to the property or earnings acquired after marriage. "The power of a husband," noted women's historian Aileen S. Kraditor, "legally extended even to the right to prescribe the medicine his family must take and the amount and kind of food they ate."[2] In the Hoosier State, the predominant attitude of men toward women might best be summed up by the remark of one of the members of the Indiana Constitutional Convention of 1850–51 who remarked that females possessed "all the rights which the Bible designed them to have in this Christian land of ours."[3]

At four years old, Mary Eliza Wright was too young to attend the Seneca Falls meeting, but she would spend her life fighting to see that her sex received the same rights as men in Indiana, nationally, and internationally. Born on 27 May 1844 in Greenfield, Milwaukee County, Wisconsin, Mary Eliza was the second daughter and youngest of four children of Philander Montague and Mary Weeks (Brackett) Wright. The girl's parents were originally both from New England and had migrated to Ohio where they met and married. Friends knew Mary, the mother, as a "sweet and charming" individual possessing as well "an unerring literary taste."[4] Philander, the father, was a former schoolteacher turned farmer. The family lived on a forty-two-acre farm described by a family member as "homely and plain and storm beat and scarred by many a stain."[5]

Mary Eliza, who adopted the name May for herself, proved to be a precocious child, reading Milton by the age of seven and receiving instruction from her father and from academies in Wauwatosa and Bloomington, Wisconsin.[6] Reminiscing about her early days in Wisconsin, May said she inherited from her family a "passion for human liberty in all its phases," as well as the knowledge that men and women were not treated equally.[7] Family legend has it that Philander Wright wished for his daughter to follow in his footsteps and attend Harvard University and therefore inoculated her with the "strong belief in the right of women to wider opportunities for education and to a fuller share in the honors and the profits of business, professional and industrial activity."[8] There were, however, limited opportunities for women in higher education in nineteenth-century America. Even those who demanded enhanced educational opportunities for women sometimes did so only in the belief that the knowledge might improve their ability to be housewives and mothers, and pupils pursued studies not in mathematics or history, but in embroidery and painting.[9]

Luckily for May, her father supported her attempts to further her education. In 1863, in order to pay for her additional schooling, she took a teaching job in the Waukesha County, Wisconsin, schools. One-room schools modeled after those of New England dominated the state's educational system during the time May taught there. Housed in crude structures (a Wisconsin historian noted that a school was considered advanced "if it had separate toilets for boys and girls") equipped with limited instruction materials, schools were led by teachers with little training. An eighth-grade education might even be enough for a person to secure a teaching job through a county superintendent responsible for certifying teachers as fit for their new responsibilities. One state superintendent even went so far as to claim that "an illiterate teacher is best for a school of beginners."[10] Like May, many teachers in Wisconsin—and throughout the country in the late nineteenth century—were young women, poorly paid, who started in the profession at age eighteen or nineteen. It was not uncommon in these country schools for a few of the students to be older than the teacher leading the class.[11]

There were a few high points in May's early days as a teacher in her home state. In a letter to a friend she rejoiced at the acquisition of a blackboard for her class. Although used and not in the best condition, it proved a better teaching tool than what she had used before: boards painted black. The blackboard and a lone elocutionary chart constituted May's classroom furniture, but she consoled herself "for the want of other, by admitting that if I had it, I might not know how to use [it]." But the grind of working all day and studying at night took its toll on the young teacher, who complained to a friend: "I am so tired that if I could only rest free from labor, care & anxiety for a few years & then be resurrected, why perhaps I might enjoy life some. And what good is my work & worry to accomplish after all? If I were to kill myself in the service of the little pests (whom for all their indifference, I can't help but loving) not one of them would 'rise up and call me blessed.'"[12]

In the fall of 1865 May left her teaching post to enter an institution that strove to offer women a higher education equal to that given to men at Harvard and Yale: the Northwestern Female College in Evanston, Illinois. May was drawn to the school, founded in 1855 by the brothers William P. and Colonel J. Wesley Jones, in part because a friend of hers, Emily Conright, had studied there. Before the Jones brothers established their college, the few institutions of higher education open to women in the Midwest were female seminaries, often derisively known as "fem-sems." The new college, said J. Wesley Jones, would strive to provide "young ladies ample facilities for a thorough collegiate education near home and amid such rural seclusion as will secure every possible guaranty for health, morals, and refinement." In spite of financial difficulties, a fire that destroyed the college's first building, and resentment from Northwestern University over the use of a similar name, the Northwestern Female College had grown by the time May entered the school into a respected place for women's education, drawing students from all over the country.[13]

An "ambitious and exacting" student, May's one-year attendance at Northwestern became for her a time of serious study of such subjects as chemistry, Latin, rhetoric, zoology, logic, and trigonometry. "In those days," she later observed of her college career, "I was a very unsociable person, absorbed in books and caring little for any other manifestation of the human spirit, so almost everyone knew more about the 'come and go' of the daily life of the college than I." She had had high praise for the school's president, Dr. L. H. Bugbee, who served in that post from 1865 to 1868. She described Bugbee as "quite a model man," although he was "sometimes sadly puzzled to know what to do with some of his 'wild charges.'" The Wisconsin native had less kind words for her "pretty & pleasant" fellow students, expressing disappointment that her classmates were not "more brilliant, more exacting of themselves and of me," and also believed that her teachers were more kind than capable. Although disappointed that the school's standards were not higher, May did admit they "were the highest that there were at the time."[14]

In 1866, May and six other women received their diplomas from the Northwestern Female College (May was awarded a laureate of science degree). The next summer, she returned to her teaching career at a school in Grant County, Wisconsin. A family scandal, however, soon found the Wright family leaving their home behind for a new life in another state. The move was necessitated by the actions of May's brother, Philander, a Civil War veteran who upon his return from the conflict had traveled to Alton, Illinois, to study medicine with an older half-brother, Charles. While there, Philander and Charles's wife, Victoria, fell in love, causing Charles and Victoria to divorce. Fearing for the family's safety and reputation, the newly married Philander and Victoria, along with May, her mother, and father, moved to Corinth (then Cody's Mills), Michigan.[15]

May found work for a time as a teacher in Corinth before moving on to Plainwell in 1869 to serve as teacher and principal at the town's high school. While in Plainwell she met Edwin W. Thompson, a mathematics teacher from Paw Paw, Michigan, whom she described—after making him shave off his mustache—as "gentle in manners, and nature" as well as possessing "a fine literary taste."[16] Thompson's friends noted that he was an "earnest apostle" on behalf of science and through "systematic thinking and indefatigable labor, reached a proficiency in the knowledge of natural things far beyond that expected of a man at his age."[17] May left Michigan in the fall of 1871 for a new assignment—teaching German at the high school in Franklin, Indiana, for $60 per month in wages.

Her hiring by the Franklin school system may have been prompted by a law passed in the state two years earlier that required township school trustees to "procure efficient teachers, and introduce the German language as a branch of study," upon the demand of twenty-five or more parents. She was also part of a trend in the Hoosier State to employ more female teachers as replacements for the often poorly trained pedagogues of pioneer days who were respected more for their physical attributes than their intellectual achievements. "If he was able to read, write, and cipher," noted Indiana school administrator George Brown, "and to whip the largest boys, he was considered well qualified for his work." Before long, however, those responsible for hiring teachers began to realize that "love and kindness were much more potent elements than force in the management of the school, and from that time women began to occupy a prominent place in the profession."[18] For example, from 1855 to 1870, the percentage of women teachers in Indiana rose from 25 to 40 percent.[19]

May worked in Franklin until late winter, when she returned to Michigan to marry Thompson on 2 March 1872. The young couple returned to Franklin in 1873, with Edwin Thompson taking over as superintendent and May becoming principal of the high school. The new administrators were working in a city that had just undergone a boom in education. A new high school, called "one of the best school buildings" in the state by one historian, had been opened in February 1871, and its former superintendent H. H. Boyce (whose wife also served as principal at the high school) had established the city's first graded school system.[20] The central Indiana community, like other towns in the state, was part of the growth and development of education in Indiana following the Civil War—a growth that placed an emphasis on "routine, order, and compliance." Although the Indiana General Assembly had passed a school law in 1852 authorizing a property tax to provide for free public education, the state supreme court, in rulings in 1854 and 1858, struck down the law as unconstitutional. "The system was practically crushed," noted Richard G. Boone in his history of education in the nineteenth state, "a fine system, with officers, houses, appliances, etc., but with no money to pay the teachers." It took the Indiana legislature until 1867 to hit on the winning strategy of reenacting the original school law in hopes that new judges on the court might view the matter in a different light. "The constitution was the same;" noted Indiana historian Jacob P. Dunn Jr., "the law was similar; but the judges were different, and so was public sentiment." The plan worked; it took another eighteen years for the law to be—unsuccessfully—challenged at the state's highest court.[21]

The Thompsons seemed pleased with their new home. "Our present position," May wrote a friend back in Wisconsin, "is in every respect preferable to Plainwell. It [Franklin] is three times as large, and our salary is correspondingly generous; besides, success here means much more than success in a town of Plainwell's size; and if we are to be teachers we have the American desire to be prominently successful ones."[22] The couple, however, only stayed in Franklin for one year before resigning to accept positions in the state's capital—May as an instructor in German and later

English, and Edwin as a teacher in the business department at Indianapolis High School. The Thompsons were joining the staff of a school that like many in the state had had a rocky start, but would grow into one of the finest educational institutions in Indiana.

The first public school in Indianapolis opened on 25 April 1853, under a code of rules written by attorney Calvin Fletcher, one of three school trustees elected by the city council. After the establishment of a graded school system in August, a high school was instiued in September. The Indiana Supreme Court rulings that struck down the local power to tax for schools devastated Indianapolis's schools and led to the departure of superintendent George Stone who took a similar job in Minneapolis. "We have no hesitation in saying," the *Indianapolis Journal* editorialized, "that we could very much better afford to lose all four of the Judges who assassinated the schools than the one faithful superintendent who made them the pride of the city and the state."[23] Gradually, however, Indianapolis reinstituted its system of free public schools, aided in no small part by the guidance of a new superintendent, Abram C. Shortridge, who took over the schools in the summer of 1863.

Shortridge, who had moved to Indianapolis in 1861 to take a teaching job in the preparatory department at North Western Christian University (now Butler University), set out to revitalize the city's schools. Although handicapped by an attack that left him blind for a time, Shortridge introduced a graded school system, increased the length of the school year from approximately three months to nine months, constructed new schools modeled on the John Hancock School in Boston, and in 1865 reopened the high school with William A. Bell as principal. In addition, he proposed, and the school board agreed, that due to the system's lack of funds female teachers should be employed because they could be paid smaller salaries than male educators. To train teachers for these positions, Shortridge established on 1 March 1867 a training school in Indianapolis where the trainees helped instruct pupils during the morning and took classes themselves in the afternoon. He also appointed a woman, Nebraska Cropsey, as supervisor of primary education for Indianapolis's schools.[24]

By 1874 health problems had forced Shortridge to quit his superintendent position for a new job as president of Purdue University. But the system he left behind continued to flourish, especially Indianapolis High School. Bell had resigned as principal in 1871 and was replaced by George P. Brown, who served until 1874, when he became the new superintendent of the Indianapolis schools. Brown had scoured the country for quality teachers to staff the high school, which was located at the northeast corner of Michigan and Pennsylvania Streets in a building originally owned by Robert Underhill and that later served as the Baptist Young Ladies Institute. In addition to the Thompsons, his talent search had also secured for the school the services of David Starr Jordan, who would go on to become president at both Indiana University and Stanford University. Jordan, who had trained under Harvard scientist Louis Aggassiz, took up science work at Indianapolis High School.

At first sight, Jordan found Indianapolis "singularly monotonous," but he soon came to love the town, among other reasons because the community "contained an unusual number of clear-headed and broad-minded citizens." Jordan spent a "pleasant" year teaching in Indianapolis, even earning some extra money by selling his collection of fish to the school for its science department. In his autobiography, Jordan mentioned a few of his colleagues at the school, including Mary E. Nicholson, William W. Parsons, and both of the Thompsons. "A favorite with all was Will Thompson," Jordan noted, "who came bringing his bride, May Wright, a woman of remarkable keenness of mind." Jordan became a friend of the Thompsons and continued to correspond and visit May in later years.[25] May also captured the attention of Indianapolis school administrator Brown, who cited her as one of the female teachers in Indiana "working with an energy and intelligence that shows clearly that the power of abstract reasoning and generalization is not limited to men."[26]

When the Thompsons first moved to Indianapolis, they lived in rooms at a house on North New Jersey Street, just off Fort Wayne Avenue, and later moved to a residence at 273 Christian Avenue. The couple soon became part of one of the city's most intellectually active neighborhoods: an Indianapolis subdivision known as College Corner. The area had been developed by Ovid Butler, an attorney, civic leader, and founder of North

Western Christian University. Butler sold part of his land holdings as the site of the new university, which was constructed from 1854 to 1855 at what is now Thirteenth Street and College Avenue. Also, in March 1862, nine blocks of Butler's land was turned into the College Corner subdivision, a residential suburb bounded by College Avenue on the east, Christian Avenue on the south, Western Avenue (now Central Avenue) on the west, and Lincoln Avenue (now Fifteenth Street) on the north. "The University prospered and remained on this site for twenty years," noted Helen McKay Steele, an area resident. "During this time the families of teachers and pupils came to live near it, doctors and lawyers found it a congenial neighborhood and so did plain people who were not professional but had a love for books and learning." The street names in the neighborhood—Ash, Oak, Vine, Cherry, and Plum—possessed pleasant connotations for residents, she added, "suggestive of sitting peacefully in the shade, or having plenty of fruit for pies and preserves." Butler ensured the district's stability by selling lots only to people who intended to build homes.[27]

The neighborhood's congenial atmosphere was also enhanced through an organization that offered its members a social and educational service during a time when entertainment activities were limited. In the fall of 1872 two Indianapolis schoolteachers, Nicholson and Mary Colgan, organized the College Corner Club, a literary society with membership open to both men and women drawn mainly from the area. "Its membership," said Martha Nicholson McKay, an early member, "has always included those, not only of widely differing views but those of different pursuits as well—judges, lawyers, physicians, men of business, women with the cares of family, and from time to time a good representation of America's nobility—teachers in the public schools."[28] Among the "nobility" mentioned by McKay were the Thompsons, as well as an old friend from Indianapolis High School, Jordan, at that time a professor at North Western Christian University. The group's meetings were known for "free discussion, literary flavor and social charm," and also included some original work by club members. In fact, Jordan, known mostly for his work in science, made his debut as a poet during his time with the College

Corner Club.[29]

Through their association with the College Corner Club, and shared membership in an early suffrage society (the Indianapolis Woman Suffrage Society formed in April 1873) and in the local Unitarian Church, a group of women in the neighborhood came together to form an organization that continues as the longest running of its kind in the state: the Indianapolis Woman's Club. The club held its initial meeting on a frigid afternoon on 18 February 1875 at the home of McKay, located at 156 Ash Street (now Carrollton Avenue).

The Indianapolis gathering did not mark the first time that women in America, or Indiana, had formed such an organization. In 1858 Constance Fauntleroy, the niece of Robert Dale Owen, returned to New Harmony after living in Europe (her family had been with their uncle during his service as United States ambassador to Naples). "Returning home when nearly twenty-two years of age, brilliantly educated, particularly in music," noted Fauntleroy's daughter, Ellinor Dale Runcie, "and with her earnest soul thrilling with a new joy, the joy of an awakened religious life, she gave herself ardently to the intellectual and spiritual service of the community." In August and September 1859, Fauntlerory, joined by other women, met in the Old Fauntleroy Home to discuss the possibility of forming a woman's club. On 20 September 1859, the women formed a reading and literary group called the Minerva Society, whose object was "the mental improvement of its members."[30]

With its constitution and bylaws penned by Owen, who had championed women's rights at Indiana's constitutional convention of 1850–51, and a motto "Sapientia Gloria Corona Est (Wisdom is the crown of glory)," the group met at one another's homes. During meetings, noted Fauntleroy, the organization's president, the society "had a reading, a short original story or poem, and discussed books or a question. The work was assigned to each member in her turn, and we often had lively discussions." Minerva members were prohibited by its constitution from speaking about the group's proceedings or business in public, and no "gentlemen spectators" were admitted. The group disbanded, however, after about three years and after Fauntleroy, tired of what she believed was a "stifling" society, married Reverend James Runcie and moved to Madison, Indiana. In 1864 she started a similar organization in her new hometown—called the Bronté Club—and served as its president for a decade before moving to California and Missouri.[31]

In spite of Fauntleroy's pioneering efforts in Indiana and elsewhere, the first models for women's clubs are generally credited to the New England Woman's Club, formed by Caroline Severance and Julia Ward Howe, and the group Sorosis, organized in 1868 by women who were unhappy about being denied attendance at a New York Press Club dinner for famed British author Charles Dickens. "We have proposed," the women announced in establishing Sorosis, "to enter our protest against an idle gossip, against all demoralizing waste of time, against the follies and tyrannies of fashion, in short, against anything that opposes the full development and use of the faculties conferred upon us by our Creator."[32]

In Indiana's capital city, McKay had been one of the twenty-four original signers of the constitution for the aforementioned failed Indianapolis Woman Suffrage Society. "The air was thick with prejudice against woman escaping from her sphere," McKay noted of the time.[33] She discovered that some in the community were also leery about joining the new women's group she proposed to form. One woman wrote McKay that she found her mission in life in taking care of her two children, and did not wish to embark on other work. Another "well-meaning woman," she added, wrote expressing her belief that McKay should be able to "see that your God-given duties point in another direction." In order to mollify these objections, McKay had to make infinite explanations about the proposed club, "giving repeated assurance that it was not the purpose to form a suffrage society, or a branch of the then newly organized temperance crusade; that its work would not be irreligious; that it was not likely to be followed by strange climatic changes or terrestrial convulsions, or immediate mental revolutions."[34] Years later she noted that the club came into being out of a "sincere desire to help women into a recognition of the possibility of reconciling intellectual and domestic work."[35]

McKay managed to coax six other women to join her in her home's parlor, a "pleasant room" decorated in typical Victorian style with a walnut, glass-door bookcase, a walnut secretary along each side of the mantel, a sofa, rocking chair, and chairs upholstered in black haircloth. A plaster statue of Dickens—the titular reason behind the formation of Sorosis—looked placidly upon the proceedings as McKay was joined by her mother, Jane Nicholson, and five other women: May Thompson, Eliza T. Clarke, Laura Giddings Julian, Belle Thorpe Manlove, and H. Kate Martin. The minutes for that first meeting, taken by McKay, record the following:

> Several ladies met at the residence of Mrs. McKay for the purpose of organizing a Woman's Club. The meeting was called to order by Mrs. McKay and Mrs. Laura G. Julian chosen to preside. Mrs. May Wright Thompson and Mrs. Belle T. Manlove were appointed to draft articles for a constitution, and while this committee was out, the chairman gave to the audience some views in relation to the object desired in the establishment of this organization. The committee on constitution reported five articles which were discussed, accepted and signed by those present. It was, however, deemed advisable to leave the election of permanent officers for a subsequent meeting.
>
> Mrs. Manlove, Mrs. Thompson, Mrs. Clarke, and Mrs. McKay were appointed to confer with certain persons, supposed to be interested, and who would be desirable members, and report to the following meeting. Mrs. Thompson was then chosen vice-president and Mrs. McKay secretary, and, after some general discussion, the meeting adjourned to meet in one week on Thursday, February 25th at the residence of Mrs. Martin and perfect the organization.[36]

The club's original constitution, written by May and Manlove, called for the group to be an "organized center for mental and social culture" for its members—a statement later modified to include the phrase "and for the improvement of domestic life." To achieve this goal, the association encouraged a "liberal interchange of thoughts by written essays and discussions upon all subjects pertaining to its objects," a common goal of the numerous women's clubs formed in America during the late nineteenth century.[37] The Indianapolis club's second meeting, held a week after its

first, saw the election of Eliza Hendricks, the wife of Governor Thomas
A. Hendricks, as president; Thompson became chairman of the club's
executive committee. To meet the goals stated in its constitution, the club
assigned as the subject for discussion at its next meeting the following:
"To be a good housekeeper, is it needful to devote one's entire time to the
work?"[38]

Although the housekeeping topic seemed to be noncontroversial, the
group endured some rough moments in its early history. Its initial
president, First Lady Hendricks, selected by May as head of the nom-
inating committee to perhaps obtain some needed eclat for the fledgling
organization, failed to attend any subsequent meetings; first vice president
Julian took over the post. A history of the club speculates that Hendricks
may have shied away from allying herself with the organization because
she feared that it "might turn out to be a suffrage society in sheep's
clothing," and she was already more interested in public affairs than literary
matters. The Hendricks incident highlighted one of the group's problems:
how could it balance the needs and desires of its more liberal, women's
rights-related members with their more conservative colleagues? "Lest our
little craft should sink in an uncharted sea," noted McKay, "the first
programs were designed to quiet the fears of the anxious."[39] These
programs included such seemingly mundane matters as the relative
advantage of selecting Tuesday instead of Monday for wash day, and hints
on how to clean silver. The more conservative club members said McKay,
herself a suffragist, were "appeased by papers on the newest discoveries in
domestic science, or the always fruitful theme of how best to govern
children." She noted that whenever the subject of how best to govern
children was discussed, those who were most prominent in the discussion
were usually those without "practical knowledge, while the mother who
had sung her baby to sleep in order to attend the club was silent."[40]

The club's early days were marked by meetings where members wrestled
over "little points in the constitution, while great and waiting questions
were passed by; days when Cushing's and Roberts' rules were exalted above
the Golden Rule," lamented McKay. The club's core, however, including
founders like McKay and May, "stood bravely by one another" to ensure

the organization's survival.[41] But by the end of its first decade of existence the club—meeting on the first and third Fridays of every month and limiting membership to a hundred individuals—found itself moving away from "the timid semidomestic programs" of its early days to dis-cussions on more intellectually vigorous topics such as English and French history. In fact, everything became a topic for debate, except for such prohibited areas of discussion as politics and religion. The group's "wisdom" in banning such content, noted McKay in 1885, might account for the organization's continued growth and vigor. (The club's proscription against discussing politics and religion continues today.) Emboldened by the group's success, club members were not bashful about touting its mission to others, even those who believed that a woman's place was in the home. Speaking enthusiastically about the club to a rabbi who happened to be visiting the city, McKay received the response: "Sarah's place is in her tent." The veteran clubwoman gaily replied: "Oh yes, we know that. We only want her to have a window in it."[42]

One of the club's original purposes was to encourage its members to broaden their minds. In a privately printed pamphlet published by the club in 1925 to mark its fiftieth anniversary, there appeared a fictional letter from Grace Giddings Julian of Irvington to her cousin, Kate Giddings of Jefferson, Ohio. In the letter Grace Giddings Julian, daughter of club president Laura Giddings Julian, wrote that her mother believed that ladies with families "need to belong to a club more than young ladies that go to college, because the young ladies have to study anyway, but the ladies like Mrs. Thompson and Mrs. McKay and Mama might not if they didn't have the club. She says they learn things at the club that they can tell their families too."[43] Organizations such as the Indianapolis Woman's Club did more than provide its middle-class members with facts and figures. These clubs served as a training ground for future leaders in community affairs and in the national battle to win for women the right to vote. Although some club members, as one women's historian pointed out, chose to enter public life "without adopting the aggressive stance associated with either the temperance crusade or the . . . movement for woman suffrage," others gladly flocked to these groups.[44] For example, the Indianapolis Woman's Club spawned such community organizers and suffrage advocates as May and McKay, as well as such future club leaders and feminists as Grace Julian Clarke, president of the Indiana Federation of Clubs and an officer for the Woman's Franchise League.

May, however, had little time to enjoy the club's camaraderie. In the summer of 1875 she left Indianapolis to join her husband at Mountain Sanitarium in Asheville, North Carolina. Edwin Thompson had contracted tuberculosis and had gone to North Carolina in hopes that the mountain climate might offer him some relief from his condition. Unfortunately, he succumbed to his illness, dying on 19 August 1875. His last request to his wife, reported the *Indianapolis Evening News*, was that "the worn out body be left among the hills." In lamenting the teacher's death, the newspaper noted that those who knew Edwin Thompson would never forget "the charm of a presence, so gentle, yet so strong, so serene and sweet as to be universally felt and remarked wherever he went."[45] His colleagues in education echoed the newspaper's praise. In a resolution honoring the former teacher, the Indianapolis school board proclaimed that in Edwin Thompson they "recognized a scholar of large attainments, remarkable for his clear and vigorous mind, a successful instructor, a kind and sympathetic friend, a genial and cheerful companion."[46]

Her husband's death instilled in May a desire to live up to his sterling character. "My husband had the purest, strongest and tenderest spirit I have ever known," she wrote a friend. "*To be with him was* my supreme joy, and now that he is gone from me, to *grow up* to the *stature* of his spirit is my one object."[47] She lost herself in her work, returning to her classroom at Indianapolis High School. But just a few years after her loss, May discovered a cause that would consume her energies for some time to come: woman's suffrage.

Chapter 2

THE SUFFRAGETTE

During the spring of 1878 Indianapolis society crackled with "mysterious whisperings" concerning a proposed meeting involving women in the community with "'advanced ideas'" about their sex. A secret summons drew ten people—nine women and one man—to a gathering at Circle Hall. Although the issue of rights for women had been seriously debated in the nineteenth state as far back as the 1850s—and Indiana had been one of the first states in the country to form a woman's suffrage organization—most respectable citizens considered the idea radical at best. "Had we convened consciously to plot the ruin of our domestic life, which opponents predict as the result of woman's enfranchisement, we could not have looked more guilty or have moved about with more unnatural stealth," said May Thompson, one of the ten people at the meeting. The conservative atmosphere that dominated Indianapolis could be ascertained from the group's taking more than two hours to discuss whether or not the new society should take a name for itself that would clearly advertise its intent.[1]

About a month after this initial meeting, twenty-six people attended a second gathering, this time at the home of Zerelda Wallace. This effort resulted in the formation of the Indianapolis Equal Suffrage Society. The society consisted of men and women "willing to labor for the attainment of equal rights at the ballot-box for all citizens on the same conditions."[2] During the next seven years, the society campaigned for its cause by holding forty-three public meetings, distributing thousands of tracts, and sponsoring talks by such nationally known suffrage advocates as Frances Willard, Susan B. Anthony, and Elizabeth Cady Stanton. Through its various parties and other activities, including literary exercises, the society, noted May, "became a factor in the social life of the city" and became the means by which the association secured for itself "greater popular favor" than it could have garnered otherwise.[3] The society needed all the support it could muster when, just three years after its founding, it petitioned the state legislature seeking the right to vote for Hoosier women.

May's work with the local association gained for her entrée into the councils of national women's suffrage groups such as Anthony and Stanton's National Woman Suffrage Association, where she served as one of Anthony's "most competent young lieutenants." Just a few months after its birth, the Indianapolis society selected May as its representative to the NWSA's jubilee convention held on 19 July in Rochester, New York, to celebrate the association's thirtieth anniversary. In the first of her many appearances on the national stage May, who gave a report on efforts in Indiana to secure suffrage for women, won plaudits from Stanton, Anthony, and Frederick Douglass. Suffragist Lucretia Mott praised the Indianapolis teacher's "strength, philosophic clearness and beauty of diction."[4] May Thompson, noted Anthony biographer Ida Husted Harper, became an Anthony confidant and one of the many "valuable workers to the cause of woman suffrage" joining the fight during the decade from 1870 to 1880.[5]

In fighting for women's rights in the nineteenth state, May followed a path blazed by such early pioneers as New Harmony's Frances Wright and Robert Dale Owen, who fought in the Constitutional Convention of 1850–51 to include in the new state constitution provisions guaranteeing a woman's right to hold property. The nineteenth state's early property laws, noted one Indiana historian, were based upon an English common law tradition that viewed women "as perpetual juveniles."[6] Owen, given a testimonial dinner for his efforts by Hoosier women following the convention, wrote Anthony that although he campaigned for property rights for women while in the legislature, he did nothing in regard to suffrage. "In those days," Owen said, "it would have been utterly un-availing."[7] Owen had a solid foundation for his pessimism. Many of his fellow delegates at the constitutional convention were appalled by his efforts to enhance property rights for women. One delegate claimed that if the convention adopted Owen's measure "it would be to throw a whole population morally and politically into confusion. Is it necessary to explode a volcano under the foundation of the family union?" Another delegate piously stated that he opposed Owen's proposition "not because I love justice less, but woman more."[8]

Even women who supported Owen's efforts on their behalf when it came to property rights were very careful to avoid such dangerous ground as seeking full political rights with men. In circulating a letter distributed to newspapers in the state calling for a memorial to Owen, its authors, poet Sarah T. Bolton and Priscilla Drake (whose husband served as state treasurer), emphasized that they were demanding only "protection for the property that Providence may enable us to give our daughters," and deprecated "the efforts of those of our sex who desire to enter the political arena—to contend with men at the ballot box, or sit in our public councils." Writing about that time, Indiana historian Jacob Piatt Dunn Jr. noted that those women who advocated votes for their sex "were subjects of almost universal condemnation and ridicule, and the great majority of women shrank from anything that savored of political publicity."[9]

There were some in Indiana, however, bold enough to consider the shocking notion that a woman should be allowed to exercise the franchise. At an anti-slavery meeting in Greensboro, Indiana, in 1851, Amanda Way, an abolitionist, prohibitionist, and licensed minister, offered a resolution declaring that women were "being oppressed and degraded by the laws and customs of our country, and are in but little better condition than chattel slaves." To help remedy the situation, Way (who when asked once why she never married replied, "I never had time") called for holding a women's rights convention. In October 1851 at Dublin, Indiana, a group of women met for a "full, free, and candid discussion of the legal and social position of women," Way noted. In a report on the "thrilling meeting" printed in William Lloyd Garrison's *The Liberator*, Henry C. Wright of New Garden, Ohio, reported that much discussion centered on whether or not women's roles as mother, wife, daughter, and sister might be degraded if they voted or ran for public office. "It was in answer that if voting and holding office would degrade women," Wright said, "they would degrade men also; whatever is injurious to the moral nature, delicacy, and refinement of woman is equally so to man. Moral obligations rest equally on both sexes."[10]

A year after the Dublin meeting during a convention in Richmond, the Indiana Woman's Rights Association was formed. Elected as the group's vice president, Way insisted that unless women demanded their political, social, and economic rights—including suffrage—they would continue "in the future, as in the past, to be classed with Negroes, criminals, insane persons, idiots, and infants." In 1859 the association presented a petition to the Indiana General Assembly, signed by a thousand men and women, seeking for women not only the same property rights as men, but also asking that the state constitution be amended "so as to extend to woman the right of suffrage." The legislature accepted the petition and passed it on to a committee, which, to no one's surprise, decided that the time was not yet right to grant Hoosier women such privileges.[11]

After this high-water mark, which included the first woman speaker (Mary F. Thomas) to appear before the legislature, the women's rights movement in Indiana came to a standstill due to an overriding national emergency: the Civil War. The Woman's Rights Association held no meetings from 1859 to 1869, years, association minutes noted, when woman suffragists were giving their time, labor, money, and even lives "to the cause of freedom for the country though ourselves still tremmeled with legal and political fetters that we had helped others to cast off."[12] The association reconstituted itself after the war as the Indiana Woman's Suffrage Association and sponsored its first meeting in ten years from 8 to 9 June 1869 at Indianapolis' Masonic Hall. The gathering received positive notices from the *Indianapolis Journal*, which noted that the assembly "compared favorably with the best that have ever been conducted by our own sex." The rival *Indianapolis Sentinel*, however, claimed in an editorial that "no amount of human ingenuity can change the arrangement of nature. When woman ceases to be womanly, woman's rights associations become her fitting province."[13]

The revitalization of the Indiana women's suffrage organization came at a time when national leaders in the fight were split on the issue of the

Fifteenth Amendment, which prohibited states from denying voting rights to people based on their race, color, or previous condition of servitude. Disagreements on this and other issues led to a splitting of the ranks into two national organizations. Led by Anthony and Stanton, the National Woman Suffrage Association focused its energies on winning women the right to vote through federal action. The less radical American Woman Suffrage Association, guided by Lucy Stone and Henry Ward Beecher, concentrated on a state-by-state approach, often working at the city and state levels to garner voting rights for women in school board and other municipal elections as a way to finally achieve full suffrage rights for women across the country. In general, the AWSA, as one women's historian noted, tended to be more conservative than the rival NWSA, striving as it did to avoid "issues that might distract from the principal objective of woman suffrage or that might alienate its majority of white middle-class male and female members."[14]

This national split caused some dissension in state organizations, including those in Indiana. At its annual meeting in 1870, the Indiana Woman's Suffrage Association narrowly agreed—by a 15 to 14 vote—to become an auxiliary of the NWSA. The Hoosier group, however, did call for a union of the NWSA and AWSA "as soon as practical." To head off any difficulties, the Indianapolis Equal Suffrage Society, according to May, held itself "aloof from all formal alliances." This stance, she said, freed the group to work with any individual or organization that had as its aim giving women the right to vote. In the years to come, the society also sent delegations to the Indiana Woman's Suffrage Association's annual meeting and representatives to conventions of both of the national suffrage organizations.[15]

In her efforts to help found the Indianapolis equal suffrage group, May had displayed the genius for organization and natural leadership ability that eventually attracted the attention of Anthony and other national suffrage leaders. May's dominant personality, however, sometimes manifested itself in unattractive ways, inspiring, as one suffragist noted, both "tender and loyal friendships and vivid aversions."[16] Her actions following the formation of the Indianapolis society drove a wedge between May and a woman with whom she had worked to create the Indianapolis Woman's Club: Martha Nicholson McKay.

In addition to her groundbreaking work with the local woman's club, McKay had been involved in the 1878 creation of the Social Science Association of Indiana and also served as a member of the executive committee from Indiana for the AWSA. It was entirely logical then that Lucy Stone, one of the American association's leaders, would write McKay in late July 1878 broaching the idea of holding the AWSA's annual meeting in Indianapolis and asking her to investigate what expenses might be involved in renting a hall and hosting speakers.[17] A few days later, McKay told her friend, May Thompson, who was on a visit to Milwaukee, the good news. In a 4 August letter to McKay, May expressed her pleasure at the prospect of having the AWSA hold its meeting in Indianapolis and offered to take responsibility for the "ways and means" of the meeting. She also pledged "to make every reasonable effort to facilitate the carrying out of their plan."[18]

Hoping to win attention for the fledgling Indianapolis Equal Suffrage Society, May, in effect, usurped McKay's role, sending an invitation to Stone inviting the AWSA to meet in Indianapolis and appointing committees to make the necessary arrangements. Stone had made matters worse by confusing May Thompson's equal suffrage group with McKay's social science organization. "I do not know how it was possible for me to get things so mixed," Stone wrote McKay. "I took it for granted it was all one society and only when your card of warning came did I get the first suspicion that we were in a trap." Apologizing for the mess, Stone informed McKay she would write Thompson to let her know that because McKay served on the AWSA's executive committee "we wish that you should be the chairman for arrangements and have a decided voice in regard everything."[19]

Stone eventually wrote to May and members of the Indianapolis Equal Suffrage Society assuring them that there was "no bad feeling or real reason for ill or disturbance of any kind on the party of anybody." She firmly stated, however, that due to McKay's standing with the AWSA, the responsibility and final decisions for the upcoming meeting was hers.

McKay had done what she had "in fulfillment of what she understood to be my request, it was not of her seeking. This is all there is of it." Hoping to heal the breach, the local society adopted a resolution expressing its regret over the misunderstanding between the two organizations. The Indianapolis society also declared that in the best interest of the cause of women's suffrage it would "take no further official action in reference to the approaching convention of said society [the AWSA] in this city, and that all committees heretofore appointed to aid in the arrangements for said meeting be discharged."[20]

In the years to come the misunderstanding regarding the AWSA meeting caused ill feelings between McKay and May. The bitterness between the two can be surmised from McKay's correspondence with Mary Livermore, a nationally noted lecturer and suffragist. Although Livermore at first demurred when asked by McKay about May Thompson's feelings about her, she did go on to relate statements made by May when Livermore declined to speak at Thompson's Indianapolis home. Livermore quoted May as saying she wished Livermore "to be entertained by some person of her selection rather than by the McKays, so that I might once, in my visits to Indianapolis, be entertained where the Unitarians and the woman suffragists *could and would call upon me.*" Thompson, Livermore continued, claimed that McKay had used her influence to keep Livermore from lecturing in order "to humiliate her." These were false charges, said Livermore, who noted:

Her [Thompson's] own letter to me caused me to arrive at that decision—her uncertainty whether or not the lecture could be made a success, joined to her evident purpose to use me against you, by demanding that I not become your guest, when I lectured the next time in Indianapolis. . . . In all her letters and speech with me, she has talked as if you were pursuing her, trying to ruin her, hunting her down. "Don't believe the stories the McKays tell you against me," she has said, and has been perfectly incredulous when I have said, "But the McKays tell me no stories against you—your name does not come up." I still feel that Mrs. T cannot harm you in any serious or permanent way. She defeats herself.[21]

May's rift with McKay did not slacken her passion for the cause of woman's suffrage. Her subsequent endeavors on behalf of women were aided immeasurably by the wholesale support of one man—her second husband, Theodore L. Sewall. Born in Ohio, Sewall had been raised in Wilmington, Delaware, where he attended Taylor and Jackson's Scientific, Classical and Commercial Academy. A member of a distinguished Massachusetts family, Theodore Sewall, at age sixteen, entered Harvard College, becoming the seventh member of his family to receive his education from that institution. He graduated in 1874, ranking fifth in a class of 158. The young man impressed Harvard president Charles Elliott, who described Sewall as "a person of irreproachable character, excellent ability and good address." In 1876 Elliott recommended Sewall to a group of prominent Indianapolis citizens who were seeking a person to serve as master of a classical school for boys in the city.[22]

Sewall opened the Indianapolis Classical School with only nine students on 25 September 1876 in a room located in an old building of the North Western Christian University at the corner of Home and College Avenues. In spite of this inauspicious beginning, the school soon won favor from the community for its rigorous course of study. The school's aim, Sewall said in a circular announcing its opening, would be "to give boys a thorough drill in Latin, Greek, Arithmetic, Algebra, Geometry and the elements of the modern languages and physical science; in short, to serve as a Preparatory School for the best Eastern Colleges." The course of study embraced all subjects that usually "precede a collegiate course, and will be arranged with reference to the highest requirements," he added, all for $100 per year (students had to provide their own books).[23] Sewall, assisted in his efforts by William F. Abbot, also a Harvard graduate, attempted to instill in his charges concern for loftier matters than just scholarship. A music teacher at the institution noted that Sewall had the firm conviction that education "without refinement and culture goes for naught. He well understood that the former with the latter is like unto an artificial flower, artistic and exquisite though the workmanship may be, the bloom, and what is more, the perfume of the flower is wanting."[24]

Sewall achieved his lofty goals for the school. Just four months after the institution opened, an Indianapolis newspaper noted that a number of "gentlemen have recalled their sons from schools in the east in order to send them to this [school], fully satisfied that the advantages are as great as those offered by any of the principal preparatory schools." [25] By the opening of the 1878–79 term, the classical school employed four teachers and enrolled approximately sixty pupils. From one small room, the school had grown to occupy an entire floor in the old university building. A reporter noted that the new rooms were "pleasant, well furnished, adorned with maps and pictures, and admirably adapted for school use; and finally, that from its location the school will attract scholars from a large section of the country, it is safe to say that before long we shall have in Indianapolis a large and thriving institution reflecting credit upon the city, upon the gentlemen who have liberally encouraged it, and upon the teachers engaged in its useful and honorable work."[26] A year later, needing additional space for its growing student body, the school moved to Harmonic Hall, located at North and Alabama Streets.

As headmaster of a thriving school, Sewall became a respected figure in the community, even winning membership in the exclusive Indianapolis Literary Club, serving as the group's secretary for a decade. Grace Julian Clarke, a friend of both May Thompson and Sewall, remembered one of the couple's first meetings at a Unitarian church service. "Mr. Sewall had recently come from Boston, a Harvard graduate, a type of the modern Puritan in appearance, retiring in manner but with a pleasant frank smile," Clarke said. "I recall seeing him go forward to meet her [Thompson] as she approached, he looking very tall and slim in a Prince Albert coat and silk hat, and she radiant in a brown silk dress . . . and a bonnet tied under her chin with a pink ribbon."[27]

After a four-year-long engagement, Sewall and May were married on 31 October 1880. In his work at the school Sewall had the assistance of a strong group of teachers, including his wife, who resigned from her teaching job at Indianapolis High School to join the Classical School staff as a German teacher for the 1880–81 school term. She later taught a class in English literature, a course that included a rigorous home reading component. The Indianapolis school board honored May's work in a resolution noting that her constant efforts to raise the standards of education in the community entitled her not only to the board's appreciation, but that of the entire city's as well. The resolution went on to say that May carried with her for the future "the best wishes of the Board and her many friends in this city for her usefulness and prosperity."[28]

In marrying Sewall, May found a perfect partner for her liberal opinions on the educational, occupational, and political status of women. "Marriage is the natural condition," May once told a reporter, "but I believe in woman living her own life and working out her own salvation in her own way."[29] Reflecting on her marriage to Sewall, May told Clarke she was thankful "to have a husband whose tastes and ideals were in entire sympathy with her own."[30] Many people who knew the couple erroneously assumed, said May, that her husband's progressive views on women dated from his acquaintance with her. "Nothing could be more incorrect," she said. "It is my proud pleasure to believe that my husband's acquaintance with me did not lower his esteem of the capabilities of women; but that esteem originated in his own fair, unprejudiced mind, and his first formal expression of it antedated our acquaintance by many years." She pointed out that at age twenty Theodore Sewall had written a college paper examining the question, "In what respects do women seem to you in our time and country to be at an avoidable disadvantage as compared with men?" In responding to the assignment, he pointed to the movement in the country for obtaining for women equal suffrage, equal education, and equal recognition in business. "I think that all these claims are perfectly just," said Sewall, "and that they will be granted sooner or later."[31]

The steady, Harvard-educated Sewall and his reform-minded wife made a perfect team. They shared the same literary and cultural interests and he encouraged and aided his wife in all her varied activities and causes. The couple's togetherness impressed their friends. Clarke recalled seeing the Sewalls at the public library before the start of their first trip to Europe, sitting together at a table "with a mountain of books before them, he calling her attention to certain things and she nodding."[32] Old friends of the couple noted that Theodore Sewall served as a "'balance wheel' to his energetic, enthusiastic, but sometimes impractical wife."[33] In the years to come the Sewalls' equal partnership became well known in suffrage circles. Alice Stone Blackwell, daughter of suffragist Lucy Stone and one of the editors for the *Woman's Journal*, wrote May in 1897 noting that the newspaper would in the year to come be featuring a series of articles on husbands of distinguished American women. She asked May to contribute an article (for no pay) on her husband. "You know that there is a popular belief that the husbands of suffragists do not amount to anything," Blackwell wrote May Wright Sewall. "We want to show the fallacy of this by writing up the husbands, especially those who really have amounted to something."[34]

With her husband firmly committed to the cause of equal rights for women, May became a leader in the fight to secure suffrage for women in Indiana. According to Sewall, the problem in the nineteenth state came not from despair at the hopelessness of the cause, but overconfidence. "We find langour of effort here," she wrote Sarah Andrews Spencer, corresponding secretary for the NWSA, "but the reason of it seems not so much a disbelief in the cause or an apathy as the belief that suffrage for women is so *sure* a thing that it is not necessary to struggle for it." She added that even if this was the general feeling, the Indianapolis Equal Suffrage Society "does feel the need of work and of workers."[35] Acting on this belief, the society in December 1880 issued a letter, signed by Wallace as president and May as secretary, to each legislator and leading newspapers in the state indicating that during the next session of the Indiana General Assembly the group would be seeking consideration of the suffrage question. "The society will petition the legislature," the letter read, "to devote a day to hearing, from representative advocates of woman suffrage, appeals and arguments for such legislation as may be necessary to abolish the present unjust restriction of the elective franchise to one sex, and to secure to women the free exercise of the ballot, under the same conditions and such only, as are imposed on men."[36]

The fifty-second Indiana General Assembly opened in January 1881 with Republicans and Democrats equally split in the House and the GOP controlling the Senate. Governor Albert G. Porter, a Republican, warned legislators that during the session women "of high mental endowments and large culture, whose lives and example, as wives and mothers, have won for them in the communities in which they live, the greatest possible respect," would ask to be heard regarding an amendment to the state constitution granting women the right to vote.[37] In fact, said May, the suffragists were determined to attack the issue on two fronts. One was to secure passage of a bill that would "immediately authorize women to vote for presidential electors." The second involved approval of an amendment to the state constitution allowing women to vote in all elections. "The immediate object," she said, "was to secure the passage of the electoral bill, for that once gained, and women by act of the legislature made voters upon the most important question, it was reasonably thought that the passage of the amendment would be thereby facilitated." To help expedite matters, legislators were lobbied by Wallace and Lafayette suffragist Helen Gougar (a person May said had "no peer among her co-workers" when it came to speaking extemporaneously), and members of both the Indianapolis and state suffrage organizations met with lawmakers "at sundry times," said May.[38]

Although the presidential elector bill, introduced by Marion County representative John W. Furnas, passed two readings in the House, it fell three votes short of making it past a third reading. The defeat came in spite of impassioned pleas on the bill's behalf by Mary Haggart and Gougar, who had first suggested that her fellow reformers seek a legal opinion on whether women—even though they were barred from exercising the franchise in state elections—might still be allowed to vote for presidential electors.[39] Failure in one area, however, did not mean the dashing of all the suffragists' hopes. The regular legislative session had expired before lawmakers had the opportunity to act on important state matters. Therefore, the legislators had to remain in Indianapolis for a special session from 8 March to 16 April. The special session gave Indiana women the opportunity to pursue their second route for obtaining the franchise: amending article two, section two of the state constitution to give women the right to vote in all elections.

On 15 March Furnas introduced a resolution in the House outlining a constitutional amendment giving Hoosier women the right to vote. The resolution passed the House by a 62 to 24 vote on 7 April and, one day later, the Senate followed suit by approving the resolution by a vote of 27 to 18. In addition to the suffrage amendment, the legislature—responding to a petition signed by 46,000 voters—also approved a constitutional provision prohibiting the manufacture and sale of intoxicating liquors. (The legislature also approved constitutional amendments fixing the term of county and state offices at four years and a requirement whereby a vote of two-thirds of the Indiana General Assembly was necessary to adopt amendments to the state constitution.) Immediately after the passage of the suffrage bill, the Indiana Woman's Suffrage Association and the Indianapolis Equal Suffrage Society invited all legislators who had voted for the amendment to a party to celebrate this achievement on behalf of woman's suffrage. Paradoxically, noted May, the defeat of the presidential elector effort had helped pave the way for the state constitutional amendment victory. "No one believed that the bill to amend the constitution would have passed," she said, "had it not been preceded by the battle over the electoral bill and the consequent education of the General Assembly in regard to this great question of political rights."[40]

The battle for woman's suffrage in Indiana, however, was far from over. In accordance with the byzantine requirements of the state's 1851 constitution, any amendment had to be passed by two consecutive legislatures and then sent on to voters for their approval. Recognizing the difficult road ahead, the Indianapolis suffrage group worked feverishly over the next few years to attract supporters to its cause. In November 1881, following a literary and social gathering sponsored by the society that included remarks by Governor Porter, May and her compatriots won another victory when the *Indianapolis Times* came out in support of woman's suffrage. "As the question is likely to become a prominent theme of discussion," the newspaper said in an editorial, "the Times will now say that it is decidedly and unequivocally in favor of woman suffrage. We believe that women have the same right to vote that men have, that it is impolitic and unjust to deprive them of the right, and that its free and full bestowal would conserve the welfare of society and the good of government." In addition to its editorial support, the *Times* in the fall of 1881 gave the suffragists a weekly column, titled "Women's Work," which May edited and wrote for the next four years.[41]

The Hoosier reformer used her bully pulpit to inform readers about various meetings and activities regarding woman's suffrage, and to agitate on issues ranging from women working outside the home to receiving advanced education. Writing about the low wages paid to women in public work, she noted many excused this inequality on the grounds that men needed the higher wages in order to support their families. "We do not believe that any person's obligations and responsibilities," May wrote, "should be the gauge of his income, rather should the latter determine the former in so far as they are subject to one's will." Even if one agreed to the proposition that a person should be paid in proportion to the number of people dependent upon them for support, she continued, further investigation could only result in increased pay for women. May pointed out that in Indianapolis, 50 percent of the 200 teachers working in the city were supporting parents, brothers, sisters, or children. "There is but one measure for wages," she said, "and that is, character, quality, and amount of work done. But if incumbrances are to be a factor let not the pay of women be abated on the assumption that they have none."[42]

In her newspaper writing May also expressed the frustrations many women felt as they fought for equal rights. She skillfully parried objections to the cause and argued forcefully for allowing women opportunities in new fields. In one column she noted that in the past it seemed as though every time women clamored for "a share in the higher labors and their rewards" of life, men would quickly assert that a woman's "delicate" physical condition prevented her from fully participating in such matters. When this objection was done away with—thanks in part to reforms in women's clothing, a cause May strongly supported—men were quick to claim women could never master the mental skills needed to become equal partners. May wrote:

The ease with which women bore away prizes and honors so soon as they had collegiate opportunity was an offset to that argument. Then sentimentality and lack of practical faculty was next urged as an argument against their [women's] possible success in the world. The steady increase of the women who can and do earn comfortable incomes awakened the fear that women, after all, had too much practical sense, and those who deprecated the growing ambitions of women urged that professional and business activity and pecuniary independence would harden woman's heart, and the very source of the world's sweetest sympathies would be dried up. But the part women have taken in the organization and administration of the associated charities system; the time and money they give to public objects; the ingenuity and devotion that they have shown in effecting schemes for the amelioration of the hard life of various classes of unfortunates, all show that culture and activity and independent means, instead of stopping the currents of sympathy, simply give them wiser direction. Thus one after another have the doubts and quibbles and false declarations of opponents been answered.[43]

Hoping to gain a legislature favorably inclined to re-passing the suffrage amendment in 1883, both the state and Indianapolis suffrage groups sponsored meetings, instituted lecture tours, and helped organize local suffrage societies. In the spring of 1882, the state association called for a mass meeting of all Hoosier women interested in having the suffrage amendment approved. Those who could not attend were asked by the group to send a postcard indicating support; the association stopped counting after receiving five thousand postcards in response. May, who presided over the meeting held on 19 May at Indianapolis's Grand Opera House, had nothing but praise for the gathering. "If any came to scoff," she noted, "they remained to participate with pride in this remarkable convention." At the time, she added, the meeting was often "referred to as the largest and most impressive" ever held in Indianapolis. [44]

That summer women, "for the first time in the history of Indiana," observed May, were used by party managers to address political meetings and attend state conventions as delegates. Suffrage proponents traveled the state to proselytize for the cause in front of Sunday school meetings, teacher associations, agricultural fairs, picnics, and assemblies of all kinds. The cause received publicity not only from May's column in the *Times*, but also from Gougar's Lafayette newspaper, *Our Herald*. "Women's influence in the campaign," Gougar wrote in her newspaper, "demonstrates her patriotism and power and her determination to be a factor in the political future of this republic in whose life she is more interested than man because in an unequal government, woman is always the greatest sufferer."[45]

To May's way of thinking, the issue of woman's suffrage was not a partisan one. "It is included," she said in her *Times* column, "in the fundamental principles of both parties." Although she admitted that there were probably relatively more Republicans than Democrats who believed in woman's suffrage, she argued it was unnecessary, and unfortunate, if it was made a partisan issue. "There are Democrats as well as Republicans among women," she noted, "and women do not wish to be bound to any party by having their cause espoused by a party as a party."[46] Unfortunately for May and her fellow suffragists, women's enfranchisement became a bitter partisan matter. At its 9 August convention in Indianapolis, the state GOP approved a resolution demanding that the suffrage amendment and the other amendments passed by the 1881 legislature be adopted and passed along for a decision by Indiana voters. "These amendments were not partisan in their origin," the Republican party noted, "and are not so in character, and should not be made so in voting upon them." The GOP called for the amendments to be voted upon at a special election to ensure "an intelligent decision thereon, uninfluenced by partisan issues."[47]

Indiana suffragists still faced an uphill battle, thanks, in part, to firm opposition to the prohibition amendment from both the Democratic party and the liquor industry. A week before the GOP convention, the Democrats had gathered in Indianapolis and indicated the party's strong stand against "all sumptuary legislation," particularly the prohibition amendment, and used its opposition to temperance as a campaign issue. The Democrats did support submitting the constitutional amendments to the people of the state for their consideration, but wanted that decision to come "at a time and under circumstances most favorable to a full vote, and therefore, should be at a general election."[48] Of course the liquor industry united in its opposition to the prohibition amendment, and also worked against the suffrage amendment because, as one historian noted, it feared that if women gained the vote, they would have enough clout to successfully enact temperance legislation. Even May acknowledged that the interests of both suffrage and prohibition supports in the 1882 campaign were identical. It came as no surprise then, that this combination of moral forces aroused the "animosity of the liquor league," she noted, "and this powerful association threw itself against submission."[49]

Feelings ran at a fever pitch during the campaign for the Hoosier legislature. Gougar, campaigning on behalf of state senate candidate and suffrage supporter W. DeWitt Wallace in Lafayette, endured threats and attacks on her character from opponents. Lafayette Police Chief Henry Mandler even started a rumor that Gougar and Wallace had committed adultery (Gougar later won a slander suit against Mandler, but Wallace lost in his try for the legislature).[50] The election proved to be a disaster for suffrage and temperance supporters, with the Democrats winning control of both the Indiana house (59 Democrats to 41 Republicans) and senate (29 Democrats to 22 Republicans). With the Democratic sweep, May said, the suffragists had "no grounds for hoping that the amendments would be re-passed and sent on to the voters of the state for final adoption or rejection."[51]

The constitutional amendments, including the suffrage and temperance measures, did not die without a fight. When the fifty-third Indiana General Assembly opened for business in January 1883, the suffragists could at least count on the support of recently elected Wayne County senator William Dudley Foulke, a firm supporter of a woman's right to vote and a temperance advocate. "If it were true that taxation without representation was tyranny, why should women be taxed and be subject to the laws and yet not be represented in making them?" Foulke asked. "The demand for woman's suffrage was really the demand for woman's liberty, for it was suffrage which, in the last analysis, framed the laws that determined how far individual liberty should be restricted by the state. The unlimited right of one class, or sex to make laws which should control the other was tyranny."[52]

During the session, Foulke submitted a resolution to the senate on behalf of the Indianapolis Equal Suffrage Society. The organization called upon the lawmakers to "submit to the qualified voters of the State, at a special election, an amendment to the Constitution of the State, giving to all its citizens, without distinction of sex, the right of suffrage." The society also asked the legislature to approve a resolution requesting Congress to vote for a federal amendment to the Constitution giving women the right to vote. In addition to the efforts of the Indianapolis suffrage group, numerous petitions were submitted to both the house and senate in support of both the suffrage and prohibition amendments. Also, the society appointed a committee, which included May Wright Sewall, Paulina Merritt, and Mary E. Newman Carey, to press for women's interests. Through this group's efforts, according to May, both houses of the legislature established committees on women's claims.[53]

Instead of risking a direct vote against the suffrage and temperance amendments, Democrats hit upon a better plan. Democratic lawmakers argued that all the proposed constitutional amendments seemingly approved by the previous legislature had in fact not been legally adopted because they had not been properly entered in the journals of the house and senate. A majority report from the senate judiciary committee examined the journals of both houses of the legislature from the 1881 session and ruled that "while said Journals show that propositions to amend the Constitution were under consideration in both House and Senate of the General Assembly, and appear to have been in some form agreed to, there is not entry . . . upon either of said Journals by which your committee can determine what said propositions were." The committee also claimed that there existed no evidence in the journals to indicate that either the house or senate "referred, or intended to refer, a proposition to amend the Constitution to this Assembly."[54]

Republican state representative Christian Holler tried again to secure suffrage for Hoosier women by successfully introducing a resolution on the issue in the house on 20 February. Although adopted in the house by a 53 to 42 vote, the senate refused to consider the matter. A frustrated Foulke, who had introduced a concurrent resolution supporting a woman's suffrage amendment to the federal constitution, complained that law-makers during the session had failed to approve "a single measure of importance to the state." He doubted if Indiana, in its entire history, could provide "an illustration of a legislature so utterly useless . . . as the general assembly of 1883."[55]

May and her colleagues were "disappointed" by the legislative defeat, "but not discouraged." The Indianapolis feminist claimed that the local suffrage society continued to "labor with undiminished zeal" and sought every opportunity to prove that women could be a factor in state politics.[56] In March 1884 May used her column in the *Times* to caution politicians that although it was a presidential year, suffragists would not be dissuaded from seeking attention for their cause. "We do not forget that during the last four years," she wrote, "we have been told that the time to appeal to the politicians would be when the two parties should again come before the country to have their respective merits passed upon by the public at large—that is, by the male portion."[57] Moving her efforts to the national stage, May was one of the speakers at NWSA's sixteenth annual convention in Washington, D.C. In her talk on 6 March, May claimed it was not "a grander thing to lead the forlorn hope in 1776, not a grander thing to strike the shackles from the black slaves in 1863, than it would be in 1884 to carry a presidential campaign on the basis of 'Political Equality to Women.'" The man who would espouse the "cause of forgotten woman-hood, and introduce that womanhood to political influence and political freedom," she said, might have the same fame as George Washington and Abraham Lincoln. The next day she appeared before a Senate committee and told the senators woman's suffrage was a "just measure," not a partisan one, due to women "by virtue of our heritage and our one father, our one mother eternal."[58]

To match her rhetoric with action, May, along with fellow Indianapolis Equal Suffrage Society member Merritt, sent a letter to Indiana delegates to the national GOP convention reminding them that there were 70,000 people in the Hoosier State who had petitioned for a woman's right to vote. "We urge you, therefore," the letter went on to say, "to consider their interests by not voting for any candidate known to be opposed to suffrage for women." The two women also presented a petition to the Republican convention's committee on resolutions demanding that Congress enact statutes to secure "equality before the law" for all citizens and denouncing the last session of the Indiana legislature for not re-passing the constitutional amendment on woman's suffrage and sending it on to voters for their action.[59]

In spite of all her efforts, May and other Hoosier suffragists found their achievements in the 1881 legislature hard to match in the years to come, with the period 1882 to 1900 being "one of uneven activity in Indiana" for woman's suffrage, as one historian noted.[60] Lawmakers friendly to woman's suffrage continued to introduce resolutions and bills in the general assembly, but were met by firm opposition. One legislator, speaking against a bill introduced in 1887 that permitted women to vote in municipal elections, said if he dared to vote for the measure his constituents "would mob me after I went home; they don't believe in sickly sentimentality."[61] There were, however, some bright spots for the suffrage cause in Indiana. In May 1887 the Indianapolis society, aided by Anthony, reorganized itself into a state organization allied with the NWSA. Gougar became president of the new state group and May served as chairman of the executive committee. The next May the NWSA held its annual convention in Indianapolis. Meeting at Rushville in May 1888, delegates from the Indiana branch of the NWSA and the AWSA agreed to merge into one state organization. Although May received a majority vote at the meeting to remain as an officer of the new organization, she refused for "personal reasons" to serve.[62]

Those personal reasons may have had to do with May's increasing role as a leader in the NWSA (she served as chairman of the organization's executive committee from 1882 to 1890). May used her organizational skills to their utmost from 1887 to 1890 when the American and National suffrage associations hammered out an agreement for a union to form the National American Woman Suffrage Association. Although the American association had little or no internal disagreements about the proposed merger, the same could not be said for the NWSA, whose members were divided on the wisdom of such a move. In her biography of Anthony, Ida Husted Harper indicated that the executive sessions on the matter "were the most stormy in the history of the association." During this time of upheaval, May remained undaunted, working tirelessly to ensure the merger. Harper noted that "only the unsurpassed parliamentary knowledge of the chairman, May Wright Sewall, aided by the firm co-operation of Miss Anthony, could have harmonized the opposing elements and secured a majority vote in favor of the union."[63]

May also traveled outside the United States to expound on the justness of the suffrage cause. On one visit to Canada she even won grudging respect from an outspoken critic of woman's suffrage, a lawyer from Halifax, Nova Scotia, named J. Murphy. In June 1897 Murphy related to Elbert Hubbard, an American writer who also happened to be a friend of the Sewalls, a debate between May Wright Sewall and himself. Talking about the debate, Murphy, an opponent of votes for women, noted that he had accepted the challenge only to avoid giving Canadian suffragists "an opportunity to crow." With the hall packed with the "finest audience" he ever witnessed in Halifax, Murphy told Hubbard that every person in the crowd must have felt he received his money's worth. "The question remains practically in the same state as it was before the debate commenced," Murphy said. He added that he regarded May as "a very clever woman indeed, and if she was more of a woman and less of a reformer and agitator I suppose my affection would be just a trifle deeper."[64]

Glory on the national and international suffrage scene did not translate into success on the state level. In the years after the two state suffrage societies merged, May increasingly came into conflict with a former ally: Gougar. The Lafayette suffragist, a frequent lecturer at meetings around the country, endured the wrath of national suffrage leaders for her flirtation with third-party politics, particularly her unstinting support for prohibition. The president of Kansas's state suffrage association had even attempted to keep Gougar from speaking in that state, which was considering giving women the right to vote. Laura Johns accused Gougar of being "a rank Prohibitionist, and she cannot refrain from talking about it in her suffrage speeches." Gougar, scheduled to give twenty speeches in the state, refused to be intimidated: "This association cannot muzzle or gag me; I have been at work in the interest of suffrage too long to allow some unknown suffragist to switch me off the track. I propose to say what I please about Prohibition in every speech that I make."[65]

Gougar had also faced similar difficulties at the women's congress held in May 1893 as part of the Columbian Exposition in Chicago. At this meeting, May had attempted to have Gougar removed from a panel on "Civil Government and Woman Suffrage." When a moderator allowed Gougar to speak, May had protested, noting that "the official board of lady managers have made an order that the voice of Helen M. Gougar must not be heard within this Woman's Congress."[66] In the following years Gougar became a focus of concern for May and Anthony and the two women shared letters plotting what to do about her. In August 1898 Anthony wrote May to complain about a suffrage meeting called by Gougar to be held in Lafayette in October. "Can the suffrage clubs of Kokomo, Tipton," Anthony asked, "be stirred up to go in numbers so as to amend the constitution—putting the [Indiana suffrage] society on a real delegate basis—and elect officers such as the *majority* prefer? I have always been sure that if only all the friends would combine or attend a meeting called by Mrs. Gougar they could rescue the society from her . . . but if all stay at home—of course she would have everything her own way—and none of the real friends can have representation in the National Association—which it seems to me is a privilege they seem to be willing to surrender to Mrs. Gougar."[67]

In her letters to Anthony, May often addressed her as "Dear General" and, like a general, Anthony could be hard on her troops. In December 1897 Anthony complained to May about the workload forced upon her by the writing of her biography, which became "like a ball and chain to me," she noted. "Some of the days I ply every single moment of both body and soul to the work of the book," Anthony said, "a good many days fully sixteen hours, take barely the time after 9 o'clock at night to put on my wraps rush around a square or two as to fill my lungs with oxygen before daring to put my head on the pillow." She went on to warn May that she and other "young folks must not talk of hard times nor the opposition of other work, nor family cares nor anything under the sun but just to push through to the best of your ability."[68] Although Anthony recognized Sewall's unique organizational talents, and often called upon her and another trusted lieutenant, Rachel Foster Avery, to plan and execute complex tasks such as the formation of the International Council of Women and other meetings and conferences, she never "strongly considered" May Wright Sewall for a high leadership position in either the NWSA or the NAWSA.[69] What stopped Anthony from placing her friend in a top post was her realization that woman's suffrage happened to be just one in a series of social reforms pursued by May during her career. For while she was engaged in the battle to win for women the right to vote in Indiana, May had also been making her mark on Indianapolis's social landscape through her leadership of what was a unique community institution for its time: the Girls' Classical School.

Chapter 3

THE GIRLS' SCHOOL

During the late nineteenth century, Indianapolis experienced a boom in both its population and industry. In spite of this, the city maintained, as historian, author, and resident Claude Bowers noted, "the charm of a large country town." Bowers, a Shortridge High School graduate, remembered his days in the capital city as comfortable ones, with the city's people living "normal lives and where businessmen went home for lunch and in the evening found time and inclination to read the [*Indianapolis*] *News* and to stroll across velvety lawns to the neighbors' to exchange views on what they read."[1] One of the most fashionable avenues in the community was Pennsylvania Street. Mary McLaughlin, who lived in a comfortable home on that street, remembered that maple trees lined the roadway, offering cool shade even on the warmest days. The street was also a place where mule-driven streetcars kindly stopped for passengers in the middle of the block, "as they never seemed to be in a hurry to get downtown."[2] Another resident of the neighborhood, Charlotte Cathcart, noted that nearly "everyone came to Pennsylvania street to walk, no matter if they lived on Delaware or Meridian."[3] At twilight the street's residents sprinkled the dirt street with water from hoses, which, McLaughlin said, "cooled everything off and made our evenings on the porch and on the lawn very happy times." The quiet nights were watched over by a night watchman, an older gentleman equipped with a whistle that he blew on every corner. Safe in her bedroom under the covers on her bed, McLaughlin often wondered if the blast of the whistle in the quiet night might "tell the thieves and robbers where he is."[4]

Although she remembered a number of famous people who frequented the neighborhood, including Benjamin Harrison and several Indiana governors, McLaughlin in particular recalled a woman whom she observed "coming up our street, often carrying a large bag of books, and walking briskly along": May Wright Sewall.[5] It was not surprising that McLaughlin frequently spied May strolling down the sidewalk, as the McLaughlin home on Pennsylvania Street was just one door down from the Girls' Classical School, which had opened in 1882 and which May ran with her husband. Until its closing in 1910, the school offered Indianapolis's female population an education equal to that found for boys in the Indianapolis Classical School and one based on the entrance requirements established for admission to such colleges as Smith, Vassar, and Wellesley. A college graduate herself, May believed that higher education was "a means to some of the largest and noblest ends, but it is also in itself a noble end. Remembering that it means a liberal education, and that such an education, if genuine, frees one's powers and liberalizes one's spirit, one must regard this intellectual liberty, which is its fruit, as a sufficient reason for desiring it, especially in the case of women."[6]

The Girls' Classical School opened with forty-four students in attendance in September 1882 on the southeast corner of Pennsylvania and Saint Joseph Streets in the former Saint Anna's school, an Episcopalian girls' institution of learning. The school, which eventually attracted to its door pupils from across the country, taught its students something different from the usual courses on such social graces and arts as painting, drawing, and music. Earlier schools for women organized in the city, such as the Indianapolis Female School and Miss Hooker's Female School, had concentrated on teaching their charges "accomplishments" rather than academics.[7] Instead of accomplishments, the Girls' Classical School offered two four-year courses of study, classic and English, with an additional year for pupils preparing for entrance examinations to college. The course also included French and German and the school emphasized that "Music, Painting, Drawing and similar branches" would not be taught. "It is intended to make this School, like the Boys School, a permanent institution, devoted to this special work, and modeled on the plan of the leading New England Academies," a catalog for the school noted.[8] May, who served as principal and also taught literature, took a firm hand in running the school. "There was no nonsense about Mrs. Sewall," one student remembered. The pupil noted that May used to come into her classroom, and after speaking a few words to Fredonia Allen, a teacher, she would then proceed to make a few observations to the students, "looking through a large magnifying glass which enlarged her eye," and which transformed her into "a Cyclops of most forbidding appearance."[9]

Even before the Girls' Classical School opened, May, no stranger to a life of intellectual rigor, had insisted that women were the equals of men when it came to a capacity for learning. In one of her columns for the *Indianapolis Times* she quoted a Dr. William Goodell of Philadelphia who reported instances of four cases of mental exhaustion, and one case of insanity, brought about by "over brain-work at school." In fact, the doctor commonly asked women who came to him asking his advice on health matters: "'Did you stand high at school.'" May had nothing but scorn for Goodell and other physicians of the time who often prescribed "withdrawal from school and cessation of all regular mental effort to all boys and girls for the varied ailments to which youthful human flesh is heir." Nearly every teacher in the country would testify that they have never had a case of a young woman breaking down due to hard study, she wrote. The real problem, she said, came about when girls age fourteen to eighteen were faced with the double role of student and society woman. Ultimately, the society role wins out over scholarship and parents withdraw their daughters from school. "She gradually regains the condition which, in a woman, people are satisfied to call 'health,'" May sarcastically noted, "and is henceforth cited as a proof that 'girls cannot endure severe and protracted mental effort.'"[10]

In opening a school with high scholarly standards, May, with Theodore Sewall's blessing and support, had given herself, as one Hoosier education historian noted, an ample "opportunity to apply some theories of her own in the education of girls."[11] One of these theories involved physical training for her young charges, a real innovation for the time, as many women's colleges only established such programs during the last decade of the nineteenth century.[12] This special attention to exercise, including gymnastics under the direction of Richard Pertuch, the physical education teacher at the Boys' Classical School, resulted in another novelty for the girls' school: a simplified dress code. May's husband might have influenced her thinking by his attempt in March and September 1881 to institute a standard way of dressing for students in the boys' school. The uniform he proposed consisted of a double-breasted sack coat trimmed with black braid and gilt buttons bearing the initials of the school. Such an outfit would, Theodore Sewall insisted, be conducive to "thorough discipline and gentlemanly manners both in and out of school."[13]

Shortly after the girls' school opened, May distributed a circular to parents and friends of the institution seeking their opinion on the desirability of adopting a simple school dress for everyday wear, which included a kilt skirt with loose waist and a sash. Such an outfit, she later noted, allowed for freedom of movement, no pressure on any part of the body, no more weight than necessary for warmth, and "quick change-ability."[14] In the circular she outlined for parents four reasons why a simplified dress should be adopted for their children:

1.   A dress with loose waist and short, light skirt is indispensable to securing the best physical results from the gymnastic exercises; and it is not probable that this dress can be secured to all the girls without the adoption of a school suit.

2.   It is believed that such a dress would discourage extravagance, and would prevent the mutual comparisons and discussions of their clothes, which often distract the attention of school girls from their proper duties.

3.   In case of the older pupils, such a dress would indicate a boundary line between school girls and young ladies in society, and diminish the temptations which beset the former to play the role of the latter.

4.   Such a dress would conduce to a community feeling among the girls, which is, in itself, an inestimable aide in securing thorough discipline, and simple, unconscious, and unaffected manners.[15]

Although May indicated that a dress code would not be adopted "unless the parents are nearly unanimous in its favor; and, if adopted, it will be compulsory upon no one to buy or wear it," she did have some immediate suggestions concerning a particular item: shoes. Those students who wore high heels made it impossible for them to participate in physical exercise, May noted. Whether or not the school dress was adopted, she called on mothers to "see that their daughters wear thick-soled shoes with low and broad heels." Later, she also warned parents that those students who wore binding corsets could not successfully or safely participate in the school's gymnasium program.[16]

There is no indication in the school's records of how many parents voted for the school uniform, but in a catalog for the institution published in May 1883 Theodore Sewall noted that early in the school's history "a loose school dress of uniform style was adopted, which has contributed largely to the ease and pleasure of the gymnastic exercises, as well as to the general health of the girls." The exercise program, he added, did much to dispel the "'nervousness' with which many school girls are, or believe themselves to be, afflicted." Sewall also praised the scholarship of the girls enrolled at the school, noting that in both the amount and quality of the work done the pupils "have shown themselves at least equal to the pupils in the School for Boys."[17]

Local newspapers shared Sewall's enthusiasm for the mental and physical vitality of the students at the Girls' Classical School. Following a gymnastic exhibition at the school on 2 June 1883 under Pertuch's direction that included march exercises, wand exercises, calisthenics, and other demonstrations, one newspaper account indicated that the exercises "were performed with a grace and ease that quite astonished even the parents of the girls."[18] After a visit to the female institution, a reporter from the *Indianapolis News* came away with the opinion that a "spirit of happiness is suffused through the school." The reporter was particularly impressed by the senior class of girls, noting the following: "They are not the kind of girls who lose their temper and self-possession under difficulties. They are not the sort of person who scream at trifles, nor do they call everything 'lovely'—cabbages, waterfalls and all—and they are not the ones who wear shoes a great deal too small when they are young, and require shoes a great deal too large when they are old. They appear permanently well poised, mentally and bodily."[19]

The poise and sophistication shown by pupils at the Girls' Classical

School came about in no small part from the no-nonsense manner in which May ran the institution. Reminiscing about their former school, students—the daughters of Indianapolis's leading businessmen and socially prominent mothers—described May as "a bit of a tyrant," whose stern visage could strike terror in their young hearts.[20] During school hours, students maintained a strict study schedule, with prescribed hours for subjects such as reading, geography, writing, spelling, arithmetic, foreign languages, gymnastics, and grammar. Known for her punctuality, May expected the same behavior in her students, often reminding them that school started at 8:30 A.M., **not** 8:31 A.M. To those who claimed they did not have the time to work out a problem or translate a sentence, May had a stock response: "You mean you did not budget your time—you had all the time there was. You wasted it."[21]

In addition to maintaining discipline while her charges were under her care, May also offered advice to parents on how students should conduct themselves outside of the classroom. In one circular distributed to parents she noted that the hours of 2:00 P.M. to 4:00 P.M. should be given over to recreation for students, but recreation of a certain type. "Mothers are requested to see," May said, "that these recreation hours are used faithfully for recreation and are reminded that visits, calls and shopping do not constitute and can not substitute recreation." She went on to say that although those in charge of the school could not regulate the social habits of students, and had "no wish to do so," they did assume that girls attempting to carry on the work of the school "will not attempt to take part in 'society' at the same time. The double role of a school girl and a society young lady can not be successfully played by one person."[22]

The strict scholarship and lofty ideals May insisted on for her students inspired and impressed many, including a Chinese prince, Pu Lun, who visited the school in 1904 while on a trip to America. John Goodnow of the American consular service in Shanghai wrote U.S. Senator Albert Beveridge that the prince considered May Wright Sewall the most wonderful person he had met on his travels. The prince asked Goodnow to pass along "his profound respects to Mrs. Sewall and his high appreciation for her work."[23] May's intensity of purpose could, however, be too much on occasion, even for someone as sure of herself as famed suffragist Susan B. Anthony. Once while visiting May in Indianapolis to discuss suffrage matters, Anthony also toured the girls' school. Writing about the incident in her diary, Anthony noted: "Mrs. Sewall introduced me to the girls of her Classical School as one who has dared [to] live up to her highest dream. I did not say a word for fear it might not be the right one."[24]

May's disciplined approach to education did pay dividends; so many students flocked to the school that in August 1884 the Sewalls announced they would be opening in the fall a new building at 426 N. Pennsylvania, which included a new primary department admitting both girls and boys at age six. The three-story, brick building, dominated by a tower rising above the main roof, included two session rooms capable of seating sixty students, two session rooms with seating for thirty pupils each, four classrooms, an office, and a gymnasium. The gymnasium was located on the building's top floor and a student remembered it being "well equipped with rings on which one could swing to the ceiling and see as far as Delaware Street."[25] Describing the new structure to its readers, an Indianapolis newspaper noted that instead of the "usual uniformity of color, the eye here is pleased by a variety of tints." The hallways and larger rooms were cherry in color, with the smaller rooms blue, salmon, olive, and amaranth in color. "Ample black-boards are provided in every room," according to the newspaper, "amounting to nearly five hundred lineal feet in the whole building."[26] By the 1886–87 school year, the Sewalls had leased a double brick building at 343 and 345 N. Pennsylvania for use as a residence for those attending the school from outside the city. M. F. Sproule, former matron at the state institution for the blind, became matron for the girls' residence, and May spent every Friday evening leading residents in "general conversations on practical and literary themes."[27]

Success carried with it certain difficulties for the Sewalls. Not everyone in the community agreed with the couples' instructional methods, particularly when it came to the exercise program. The program may have even caused the school to move from its location at the former Saint Anna's school for girls. According to one account, when a new Episcopalian bishop came to town, he was "shocked to find that a gymnasium had been installed in the church building," and took it back for church use.[28] The school's insistence on physical training for girls also came under attack in November 1889 when Noble Butler, a lawyer and leading civic figure, wrote the Sewalls to say he did not want his daughters to take gymnastics and protested paying a two dollar fee that covered an examination ("strength test") given to every girl who participated in gymnastics. In a carefully crafted, nineteen-page response to Butler, Theodore Sewall cut to the heart of the matter when he surmised that it was the gymnastics program itself, and not the fee, that constituted Butler's true concern. Sewall wrote:

> I do not think that your daughters, or any other pupils, consider themselves 'under a ban or proscription' because they do not take the gymnastic courses. There is no cause for any such feeling, other than the knowledge that Mrs. Sewall and myself are believers in physical training . . . and that we always regret it when pupils (or parents) will not accept the benefit of such training. To the best of my knowledge and belief the right of individual judgement in this matter has always been freely and courteously conceded by all persons in authority at the school. Similarly, if a parent should object to our method of teaching English Literature, or solid geometry, or zoölogy, we should never discriminate in any way against a pupil who did not take those subjects in consequence of such objections; (altho', of course, failure to take them might render the pupil ineligible for graduation, which is not so in case of the gymnastics).[29]

Sewall, who had sold the Boys' Classical School to L. R. Baugher that summer to concentrate his attention on the female institution, went on to tell Butler that as far as he could tell, all institutions that pay any attention to systematic physical training had adopted the same system as the Girls' Classical School. In examining catalogs for such schools of higher education as Yale, Harvard, Wellesley, Smith, Bryn Mawr, and Williams, Sewall said, physical training was in place along the same lines as practiced by the Indianapolis institution. "We adopt the system," he wrote Butler, "because it is believed to be the very best at present known. The practice of turning girls into a gymnasium full of special apparatus, without knowing what pieces of it they can safely and profitably use, is, and can be, advocated by none." Even if Butler did not approve of the strength testing, Sewall said he could not believe that the lawyer wished for the Sewalls "to abandon, to overturn, the whole system of physical training (to which we have given our thought and our best judgment for many years), simply because one of our best friends think we are mistaken." In fact, Sewall noted, Butler was the only parent who had expressed "dissatisfaction with the present arrangement." He invited Butler to come to the school and witness the gymnastic class at first hand, or call upon the couple at home for a consultation.[30]

If Butler took Theodore Sewall up on his invitation to visit him and his wife at home, the attorney would have been just one of a number of leading figures from the community, and the world, who visited the couple over the years. The Sewalls, who shared what some observers likened to an "idyllic companionship" comparable to that of poets Robert and Elizabeth Barrett Browning, turned their home (first on New Jersey Street and later at 343 N. Pennsylvania) into the literary and cultural center of Indianapolis. Every Wednesday the couple sponsored discussions in their drawing room, described as "a blue and terra-cotta retreat that can be extended to the magnificent length of seventy feet." There anywhere from one hundred to two hundred people gathered to ponder topics of the day. "No invitations are issued for these affairs," noted a reporter who profiled May Wright Sewall for a leading American magazine, "for it is intended than any one, irrespective of bank accounts, may air his opinion or ride a pet hobby." Hoosier writer Booth Tarkington, a longtime friend of the Sewalls, noted that those who gathered for the discussions always found May "equal to any strain put upon her by her celebrities or by ourselves. She talked 'quite wonderfully' (as the phrase goes) and always readily— nearly always smilingly, too; and with an urbane cadence which could, when necessary, produce, without ceasing to be urbane, the effect of spirited vehemence."[31] For these occasions May could also be counted upon to brew tea for those assembled, and made bread and preserves that were the envy of other Indianapolis housewives. "I really love my teacups more than many women love their husbands and children," Sewall mused, "if I may judge by the consideration I show them."[32]

The Sewalls' "tramp chamber" (guestroom) also served as a temporary haven for the numerous visitors entertained by the couple during the years they were married. Visitors ranged from suffragists such as Anthony, Frances Willard, Ida Husted Harper, Anna Shaw, and Lucy Stone, to writers Hamlin Garland, Elbert Hubbard, and Tarkington, to even traveling thespians such as Otis Skinner. The actor, who described May Wright Sewall as "a woman of rare culture, highly intellectual and vitally interested in the higher education of women," noted that she always made theater people welcome in her home.[33] Those who partook of the Sewalls' hospitality were asked to sign a register noting their stay, but were asked to put no personal compliments in the book. "Friends disobeying this command," the couple warned, "will not be invited again to sleep under our roof." [34] Most visitors, however, cheerfully ignored the Sewalls' admonition against flattery and filled the register with their thanks and good wishes. One visitor noted in the register that nowhere else "have I so felt the versatility of her [May Wright Sewall's] powers and the greatness of her loving heart, as in this dear Home where her generous and thoughtful husband makes life so full and complete."[35]

As well as serving as a social center for Indiana's capital city, the Sewalls' home also became a launching ground for a number of organizations that made their mark on the community, including three groups still in existence today: the Art Association of Indianapolis, the forerunner of the Herron School of Art and the Indianapolis Museum of Art; the Propylaeum, home to a number of women's organizations; and the Contemporary Club, a literary group open to both men and women. Although busy with the affairs of the Girls' Classical School and her commitments to woman's suffrage, May still found time to play a critical role in the formation of each of these Indianapolis institutions.

In the case of the art association, it started with a lecture. In the winter of 1881 May invited Nancy H. Adsit of Milwaukee to Indianapolis to give a series of illustrated lectures on ceramics. Adsit's visit produced a positive enough impression that she returned two years later for another art lecture, this time covering engraving and etching. At the lecture's end, May asked those present who were interested to meet at her home to discuss the possibility of organizing a society to study and promote art. Such a task had been accomplished before in Indianapolis. In 1877 the Indianapolis Art Association had been established to display the work of such local artists as Jacob Cox and T. C. Steele, but the group disbanded after only one exhibition. Also that year James Farrington Gookins and John Washington Love, both foreign-trained artists, opened the Indiana School of Art. Although the school only lasted for two years, its pupils—including future Hoosier Group member William Forsyth—refused to give up on their work and formed the Bohe [Bohemian] Club.[36]

May's proposal, she noted, received "a cordial response," and in early March 1883 a committee of ten people was selected to write a constitution for the group. After holding ten "hard-working meetings," as May noted, the committee produced a constitution adopted at a public meeting at the Denison Hotel on 7 May 1883. The group formally incorporated itself that October with Albert E. Fletcher (son of noted Indianapolis attorney Calvin Fletcher) as president and May as recording secretary. From its creation the Art Association of Indianapolis had intended to have an equal number of men and women in its membership, but found that women dominated its board of directors in its early years. May had an explanation for this disparity: "In a relatively new community, largely devoted to manufacturing and commercial interests, the number of men in whom taste and leisure for official service in such an organization combine is small." The association had as its aim the cultivation and advancement of art in all its branches, including art instruction and lectures on the subject. Also, realizing that "the art instinct 'grows by what it feeds upon,' and that people can learn to love art and to distinguish between the good and bad in it only by seeing what is good," May said, the association worked as well to establish regular exhibitions.[37]

For assistance in organizing its first exhibition, the association turned to Sue M. Ketcham, a local artist and a former student in the Gookins and Love art school. To secure paintings for the exhibition, Ketcham traveled to Chicago, Detroit, and New York, eventually gathering 453 paintings representing the work of 137 artists. The art association held its first exhibition from 7 to 29 November 1883 in a room at the English Hotel. The display, one local historian noted, "was a decided success," with attendance "increasing steadily to the last." From the exhibit, the association purchased two paintings—Harry Chase's *Running for an Anchorage* and Percival DeLuce's *The Anxious Mother*—as the first items for its permanent collection. Buoyed by this success, the association two months later opened an art school with Ketcham and Charles F. Mc-Donald of the Chicago Art League as teachers. May, along with Anna Dunlop and Henry S. Fraser, worked to manage the school's business affairs, but their efforts were for naught. "The school continued but two years," May said, "and the minutes of the Association for this period are very gloomy reading; the teachers were efficient and devoted, the business management hopeful and untiring; but without proper quarters, without endowment, without material, the school could not be maintained longer; and the year following its close special entertainments were given under the auspices of the board to liquidate the debts incurred by the school."[38]

With the burden of debt from the school hanging over its head, the association did not organize an arts exhibition in 1884, but revitalized the display the following year. The association's exhibition, "The Hoosier Colony in Munchen," featured work from a group of Indiana painters, including Steele and Forsyth, who had been studying in Munich, Germany. The catalog for the exhibition featured illustrations from members of the Bohe Club. The display, and the talent displayed by the Bohe Club in the catalog, "stirred the local pride of Indianapolis," said May, "and aroused in it a recognition of the possibilities of its own people in art." The association's exhibition became an annual event and an important date on the community's cultural calendar. In addition to the annual exhibition, which over a twelve-year period displayed more than four thousand paintings, the association sponsored other displays highlighting such works as etchings, engravings, pottery, carvings, tapestries, fabrics, embroideries, and architectural drawings. Also during that same period, May said the association offered six courses of lectures, translating into twenty-four separate talks. In 1891 the association assumed management of an art school started two years before by Steele and Forsyth, a school the group operated until 1897.[39]

During all this time the association operated without a permanent headquarters. Monthly board meetings were held at private residences and meetings involving the membership were usually convened at the Denison Hotel. Thanks to May's "fertile brain" and the devoted work of other women in the community, however, the association and other organizations in late-nineteenth-century Indianapolis soon had a facility tailor-made for their activities: the Propylaeum. This cultural oasis for the community, whose name means "gateway to higher culture," had its beginnings in a trip made by May to her former home, Milwaukee. While in the city she delivered a talk before the local woman's club, which had built the Milwaukee Athenaeum through the formation of a stock company. Inspired by their example May, upon returning to Indianapolis, related her plans to her husband and secretary, Julia Harrison Moore, during dinner. Moore later recalled the following conversation:

> As she talked, Mrs. Sewall said, "Theodore and Dewie (her pet name for me), I thought all the way on the train of a plan for the Indianapolis women. We can build and operate a Club House right here, we could sell stock enough to build it, could locate it centrally (I have thought of the place), and we can make money, for all the clubs will rent of us, the [Indianapolis] Woman's Club will have a definite home instead of wandering from one Church parlor to another, and it will eventually become a centre of culture for the city." She became more and more enthusiastic as Mr. Sewall asked her rather satirically many questions to bring her out. Finally she said: "I shall talk with Mrs. Frederick Chislett and if she approves, I shall call a committee of women and lay the plan before them." Naturally, I being too young to have any opinion, but full of amusement, said nothing, but Mr. Sewall shook his head and exclaimed, "Well, it sounds quite wild to me, but I don't doubt you will do it, if you have your mind on it."[40]

May's enthusiasm for the project soon inspired others to act, but it took some doing. On 30 April 1888 the Indianapolis Woman's Club appointed a committee of seven women—May, Elizabeth Pierce, Helen Holman, Mary Walcott, Harriet Foster, and Carrie Milligan—to find the organization a suitable room in which to hold its meetings. May, who served as chairman, shocked others on the committee, Chislett remembered, by boldly stating the group should at once reorganize itself to consider "the feasibility of forming, among the women of Indianapolis, a stock company for the purpose of erecting and owning a building which should be specially adapted for the use of the various clubs, literary, artistic, and social, which are so numerous among us." May later said that she was inspired to suggest such a venture by the work of other women who had successfully constructed buildings, including the Milwaukee Athenaeum, the Ladies' Library Association of Kalamazoo, Michigan, and the Woman's Club of Grand Rapids, Michigan. The members of the Indianapolis Woman's Club committee had serious doubts about such an endeavor, questioning whether such a scheme would be possible and wondering whether or not enough women could be found to make such a project work. Displaying her usual force of character, May calmed the committee's fears by firmly exclaiming: "Ladies, this thing will be done. If you do not take hold of it others will."[41]

During the next two months the committee met ten times and invited a total of eighty-nine women to three of those meetings, at which its plans were unveiled for the stock company's formation. "By some the scheme was considered wild and impracticable," said Chislett, "by others it was received with enthusiasm; on the whole the committee were sufficiently encouraged to go forward." On 6 June the committee incorporated itself as the Indianapolis Propylaeum and issued $15,000 in stock. Chislett said the committee selected the name Propylaeum because members wished that the building would be "the portal through which many would enter, and find their way, at least, to the outer courts of the temple of art, science and all wisdom." In incorporating itself, the Indianapolis Propylaeum claimed as its object the promotion and encouragement of literary and scientific purposes. It also included an article limiting the purchase of stock to women only. The article was not written to exclude men from the project, Chislett said, but because women involved in the project wanted "the pleasure of saying to our husbands, brothers and sons, our building is at your service, as yours have always been at ours; come often and enjoy it with us."[42]

Sixteen days after its incorporation, the Indianapolis Propylaeum held a meeting at Pierce's home and offered shares of stock at $25 each to other women in the community. Thirteen women took advantage of the opportunity to become involved in the project, and in addition a board of directors was selected numbering fifteen people. On 26 June the board met and elected Sewall to serve as president, Chislett as vice president, Holman as secretary, and Pierce as treasurer. In addition to her duties as vice president, Chislett served as one of three members of a committee charged with selecting a proper location for the Propylaeum. Examining possible sites, the committee looked for a central location with easy access by streetcars, yet at the same time "removed from the noise and bustle of business," Chislett said. They found such a site at 17 East North Street, land located on the south side of North Street, between Meridian and Pennsylvania Streets, and opposite the Indianapolis Blind Asylum. The sale of the land, owend by Alex Metzger, was finalized on 12 December 1888 for $5,500.[43]

With a site chosen, the Propylaeum board appointed a seven-member committee, which included May and Chislett, to oversee construction. From the first, said Chislett, the committee had as its goal "a thoroughly substantial, well built structure, free from all shams or pretence, and for this end no expense was spared." Plans for the building included a dining room and large kitchen, two parlors capable of seating 200 people, and a second floor assembly room with room for 600 people. The committee hired the local architectural firm of Scherrer & Moore and spent more than a year discussing and studying plans for the building. "It soon became very evident to us all," Chislett noted, "that in order to have a building at all commensurate with our needs, we must have more money at our disposal."[44]

The Propylaeum's board of directors agreed with the committee's suggestion, and recommended to its stockholders in May 1889 to increase the capital stock from $15,000 to $20,000. The stockholders agreed to the change and by 10 March 1890 all of the stock had been sold. Funds from the sale were sufficient to hire a contractor, Jungclaus & Schumacher, and the cornerstone for the building was laid in a ceremony held on 8 May 1890. May said that underlying its visible support of stone and mortar, the Propylaeum was a spiritual and ethical structure made possible by "the love, the hope, the modes aspiration, the social instinct extended, refined and elevated into the conscious social principle, and the growing faith in itself and in its power to serve humanity, which constitute modern, self-respecting womanhood—this subtle substance it is which is the substructure of this building."[45] The only hitch in the cornerstone laying occurred when Dr. Joseph S. Jenckes, former pastor of Saint Paul's Episcopal Church, who officiated at the ceremony, threw a nickel into the hollow cornerstone. A young boy darted out of the crowd, grabbed the nickel, and ran. Jenckes immediately took off after the miscreant, the tails of his black coat flying behind him as he ran. The minister managed to overtake the boy, retrieve the coin, and replace it in the cornerstone.[46]

The Indianapolis women's lofty hopes for the Propylaeum were almost dashed by a concrete fact: the group did not have enough money to construct and build the structure "in the substantial manner required," Chislett said. May broke the bad news to stockholders at the group's second annual meeting just four days after the cornerstone had been laid. Acting to secure the necessary funds for completing the project, the stockholders authorized the board of directors to borrow up to $10,000, a sum the group managed to secure from the Crown Hill Association. With the financial crisis averted, the board appointed a three-member committee, which included May, to supervise construction. Chislett marveled at May's dedication, noting that she made daily visits to the site and "watched every brick, stone and board as it was placed in position; she has made an exhaustive study of plumbing, furnaces and drainage; she has borne with unruffled temper the many annoyances that belong to such an under-taking; she has smoothed over many difficulties by her tack and for-bearance; she has induced the contractor to give us of their best, more that we dare to say that there is no building in this city more completely and thoroughly well built in all its parts . . . than the Propyaleum."[47]

The Propylaeum was formally dedicated on the evening of 27 January 1891. The eight hundred people gathered for the ceremony included stockholders and guests, presidents of the city's clubs, Governor Alvin P. Hovey, Mayor Thomas Sullivan, and representatives from the three women's organizations previously cited by May as serving as the inspiration for the efforts to construct the Propylaeum. In her presidential address, May made some sly digs at the male sex, noting that in her work seeing to the building's construction she found the average man, "as charmingly unconscious of the value of time in the matter of engagements, and as bewitchingly incapable of regulating his movements by the clock and the calendar as any woman living." Turning to more serious matters, she said the Propylaeum would serve the community as a portal, giving men and women opportunities for meeting at the highest intellectual level, dis-pensing between the two the "hospitalities of thought as well as those of the table." Over time, the building would come to be "the center of all those influences which make for culture."[48]

Just two days after its dedication, the Propylaeum hosted its first club, the Matinee Musicale, which presented a program and reception. Other organizations quickly followed suit, including the Indianapolis Literary Club, the Portfolio Club, the Dramatic Club, the Art Association, the Indianapolis Woman's Club, and a group organized at the Sewalls' home just six months before the Propylaeum opened—the Contemporary Club of Indianapolis. May envisioned this literary and social club as providing something unavailable in the city at that time: membership open to men and women on equal terms with "no excluded subjects, no forbidden ground." May, who served as the organization's first president, noted that prior to the Contemporary Club's formation, the only opportunity women in the city had to meet men on equal terms intellectually came at the Indianapolis Literary Club's ladies night. Women in the community were always assured, she added, that "ladies nights were relatively dull nights, that the members were hindered from talking their best by the em-barrassment occasioned by the infrequent presence of ladies or by the chivalrous consideration of our feebleness." The Contemporary Club held its first meeting on 25 September 1890, with John M. Coutler, a Wabash College professor and botanist, lecturing on the subject "The Physical Basis of Life." Through the years the club heard talks by such noted speakers as historian John Clark Ridpath, writer Hamlin Garland, artist Steele, politician William Dudley Foulke, and reformer Jane Addams.[49]

Both May and Theodore Sewall received praise for their contributions to Indianapolis's educational and cultural life. There were some, however, who viewed the couple as being too dominant a force on the community. One of these dissenters was Meredith Nicholson, later a well-known Indiana writer and diplomat, who expressed his disdain of the Sewalls in a 5 October 1893 letter to his friend May Shipp. In his letter Nicholson, then a staff member of the *Indianapolis News*, claimed there were "hopeful" signs that the Sewalls' influence on the city's life was waning. He noted that the Girls' Classical School had fewer students graduating that fall than in previous years, and that a number of people, including himself, had resigned from the "Contemptible Club." He went on to note:

> It was substantially stated at a committee meeting of gentlemen who were at least respectable that the male owner [Theodore Sewall] of the Pennsylvania Institute [the Girls' Classical School] was not a proper person to invite to a banquet table.
>
> At a meeting of the directors of the Dramatic Club the Sewall propaganda was denounced and it seems likely that the absurdity of the Sewall hierarchy will eventually result in the casting out of that silly group of pretenders.[50]

May may not have known about Nicholson's scornful attitude toward her and her husband, but she did realize that there were those in the community who resented her visibility, influence, and sometimes dominating personality. Mary McLaughlin, the Sewalls' neighbor, recalled that as a young girl she was out walking with her mother when the two met May, who stopped to talk to them as she often did. "Like most well-known and prominent people in the school life and club life of our city,"

McLaughlin said, "she [Sewall] was criticized very severely, for things she probably never did or said." McLaughlin noted that her mother always defended Sewall. Perhaps knowing of her friends' dedication, Sewall once unburdened her frustrations on McLaughlin's mother, lamenting: "I cannot walk down this street without being misunderstood."[51]

The Indianapolis educator and reformer faced a far greater challenge than the occasional sniping of enemies in the early 1890s when she learned that Theodore Sewall had contracted tuberculosis—the same disease that had killed May's first husband, Edwin Thompson. His illness even caused Theodore Sewall to suspend for a time his teaching and other duties at the Girls' Classical School, as his doctor advised him to travel to New Mexico in search of relief.[52] As May continued to worry about her husband's health in the spring of 1895, she received news of an unexpected gift that would change the work of the Art Association of Indianapolis from "a dragging struggle to gratifying achievement."[53]

On Monday morning, 13 May, she received a visit at the Girls' Classical School from Ambrose P. Stanton, a local attorney and her friend for the past twenty years. His first words to her were: "You are the president of the art association, I believe." Affirming her position to Stanton, May added: "And you have come to bring a fortune." An astonished Stanton then informed her that John Herron, who had dabbled in real estate and lived in Indianapolis for fourteen years before moving to California, had died in a fire on 2 May in Los Angeles. In his will, Herron had left the bulk of his estate, approximately $225,000, to the art association to establish and maintain an art school and gallery named in his honor. "Mr. Herron had long wanted to endow some kind of an institution," said Stanton, who served as executor of Herron's will. "He was not an expert in his scrutiny of art, but loved to look at pictures and selected the Indianapolis Art Association as the beneficiary of his money."[54]

On 25 May the officers of the art association held a public meeting at the Grand Opera House to share the news of the Herron bequest and, as May noted, to see if "other citizens might be stimulated by Mr. Herron's example to become in a noble sense promoters of art in this community." The association's joy turned out to be short-lived, however, as a group of

Herron's distant relatives contested the will. Also, as May observed, the association had to fence with both attorneys and legislators "who thought to make either fees or political capital out of abetting the contestants of the will."[55] Already bruised by the battle over the Herron bequest, May faced a much greater tragedy when Theodore Sewall, finally succumbing to his illness, died at home early in the morning on 23 December 1895. The respected Indianapolis educator had returned to Indianapolis shortly after Thanksgiving after a stay in a sanitarium in Poughkeepsie, New York. "A few days after his return," the *Indianapolis News* said in its obituary on Sewall, "he became so much worse that he was forced to take to his bed, and he continued to sink." In his last message passed on to the students of the school he started with his wife, he said: "Tell the girls that to be well and to be at work are the two conditions of happiness."[56]

Theodore Sewall's death meant, as one friend of the couple noted, "the desolation of one of the happiest, most perfect homes ever made by two mortals." A devastated May sent a telegram to her friend and suffragist leader Susan B. Anthony with the simple statement: "Dear General, my Theodore is taken." Anthony wrote her back telling May to "be brave in this inevitable hour; take unto yourself the 'joy of sorrow' that you did all in mortal power for his restoration, that his happiness was the desire of your life; find comfort in the blessed memories of his tender and never-failing love and care for you in all these beautiful years."[57]

May was so overcome by her husband's death that she was unable to attend a memorial meeting held in Theodore Sewall's honor on 6 January 1896 by the members of the Girls' Classical School and its alumnae association. Ella Laura Malott, an 1891 graduate of the school, re-membered that when students failed to reach the high standards set by Theodore Sewall, they could feel "his silent disappointment" and vowed to try harder next time. When pupils did meet his high standards, Malott said they were "rewarded by his silent look of approval. His silence then expressed more to us than countless words of praise." May did submit her memories of her husband's life and career for the service. She noted that during the last years of his life he found comfort in the works of Homer, Herodotus, Pliny, Cicero, and Horace. In reflecting on Theodore

Sewall's qualities, she cited "his perfect courtesy, his flawless honor, his absolute truthfulness, his tireless industry, his exacting accuracy, his respect for detail, his fine sense of the appropriate." Although May said she was "almost overwhelmed by the measureless depths of unspeakable sorrow," she vowed to be back at the school as soon as possible to continue the work started by her husband.[58]

Theodore Sewall's death caused many in the community to question whether or not the Girls' Classical School could survive. To quell persistent rumors that the school might be sold, May sent a letter to parents and alumnae indicating the rumor "has not now, nor has it ever had, the slightest foundation." Her husband's death, she went on to say, made her more determined than ever "to do my utmost to mature and execute the plans we had made for the continuance and permanence of the school."[59] In the spring of 1896 May also mailed out letters seeking references from several well-known men in the community. "I think the school was never on a better basis than at the present time," she wrote. "I feel it due to you to make this statement, for I should wish you to feel that in giving the school the support of your name as a reference, you were giving it to the support of a strong and worthy institution."[60]

Immersing herself in work, May seemed to be trying to forget the pain of her beloved husband's death. But at home Theodore Sewall was never far from her mind. Her devotion to him could seem extreme at times to others. One incident in her Indianapolis home even presaged May's attempts to make contact with her husband through spiritualist means. Dining at her home one evening, actor Skinner, a frequent guest, noted at the head of the table stood a chair that had often been the place where Theodore Sewall sat. The chair was empty now, however, except for a pot of ivy. "If she [May] referred to Mr. Sewall," said Skinner, "she would turn to the chair with an affectionate gesture as if he were present. A ghost at the feast could hardly have been less grewsome [sic] than the pot of trellised ivy." Because May allowed no alcohol to be served at her table, Skinner had to be content with calming his "edged nerves in draughts of iced water."[61]

Even without her husband's accustomed steady hand and strong support, May, as principal of the Girls' Classical School, continued to expand the institution's offerings, including offering adult education classes and starting a new Department of Industrial Domestic Science with courses on chemistry and physics as well as cooking.[62] She also remained active in civic affairs, particularly with the art association. In October 1897 the association disposed of claims from Herron's relatives challenging his bequest. Finally, in March 1899, a committee appointed by the association, which included as members May, Stanton, and C. E. Hollenbeck, devised a plan for dividing the Herron bequest into three funds: $150,000 for the art treasure fund, $10,000 for the art school fund, and $65,000 for a building and grounds fund. From April 1899 to January 1900 the association considered a number of sites in the city for an art building before finally deciding to purchase for $50,000 the Talbott property (also known as the Tinker House) at Sixteenth and Pennsylvania Streets (the building had been used by Steele as an art studio since his return from Munich). The association occupied the property on 11 February 1902, and a month later the John Herron Art Institute was formally opened to the public.[63]

Three years later, after much wrangling over cost and location, May had the honor of digging the first spadeful of dirt for a new museum and art school for the association, which was designed by the Indianapolis firm of Vonnegut and Bohn. Two days later, on 25 November 1905, the association laid the cornerstone for its new structure. It was an auspicious occasion for the association, but May noted that the public did not share in the group's enthusiasm for the project. Expecting a large throng to attend both the cornerstone ceremony and a public program preceding the event at Mayflower Church, the association board had secured a large contingent of police to help with crowd control. "The result was that twelve solemn gentlemen in uniform guard the wraps of the three ladies bearing a part in the program rendered at the church," said May, "and afterward served to swell to apparent dignity the little body of faithful members who acted as the president's bodyguard while she used the trowel." She added that the association's directors were "too elated" by the fact that a new facility was being built to feel any chagrin about the public's apparent indifference.[64]

Success with the art association came at a time when May experienced financial setbacks with the operation of the Girls' Classical School. In 1903 she confided to Anthony that she had experienced some "sad disappointments in regard to the non return of some pupils none of them, however, because of dissatisfaction with the school, but I am relying upon unexpected accessions to balance counts."[65] The drop in student enrollment came about from increased competition from the city school system, which had added Manual High School in 1895, and from a former teacher at Sewall's school, Fredonia Allen, who in 1902 had started a rival institution, Tudor Hall School for Girls (now Park Tudor School). In May 1905 May announced that she had entered into a partnership to run the Girls' Classical School with Anna F. Weaver, a former student at the school and a graduate of Stanford University. Weaver, May informed friends and patrons of the school, would share with her "all the responsibilities, financial as well as executive, and in every way having equal authority and equal responsibility." Pointing out that the school had graduated 226 women since its opening, with 93 of those going on to colleges and university, May stressed that the addition of Weaver to the school would serve to be "a source of every kind of strength,—intellectual, moral and financial." She also expressed the hope that the school might make the change from "a purely private enterprise into an endowed institution."[66]

The partnership continued for two years, but by late February 1907, May decided to retire and sell the school to Weaver, who moved operations into the double residence on North Pennsylvania Street. May sold the school building to the College of Musical Art for $20,500. Weaver continued to run the school until 1910, when it closed for good. In a letter May sent to graduates of the school informing them of her intention of retiring at the end of the school year in June, she noted the following:

> An entry in my diary, made the night before The Classical School opened in 1882, runs thus: "To-morrow I commence a work to which I now expect to give the chief part of my life for twenty-five years."

This I have been permitted to do. This entry shows that it was within my intention to give only twenty-five years to this particular method of carrying out my educational ideas. For this opportunity I am profoundly grateful. Persistent adherence to this work has resulted in advancing my own education. I hope that I have not been the only one profited by my efforts, but that you also feel it *is* good for you and that it *will continue* to be good for you to have had and to continue to have this intimate relation with my life.[67]

May's retirement from the girls' school was front-page news in Indianapolis newspapers. The *Indianapolis News* reported that the educator did not know what she might do in the future, but had received "several offers in literary and lecture fields."[68] With her retirement, May also began distributing to various institutions in the city the numerous books, articles, and artwork she had collected over the years. She gave the local library 300 books; a number of reports, pamphlets, and magazines; and programs from clubs from throughout the United States and around the world. The art association received May's collection of Mexican pottery and art catalogues from galleries she visited on her travels.[69]

By clearing her home of these items, May was saying farewell to a community she had served well since she had come to teach at Indianapolis High School in 1874. She left Indianapolis in the summer of 1907 to give lectures at Green-Acre-on-the-Piscataqua in Eliot, Maine. Established by Sarah Jane Farmer in 1892, Green Acre held conferences each summer on various aspects of religion and philosophy that featured such nationally known speakers as Edward Everett Hale, W. E. B. DuBois, Booker T. Washington, John Greenleaf Whittier, and William Dean Howells.[70] Even before she had left Indiana for Maine, May, and her genius for organization, had won fame far beyond the borders of the nineteenth state through her work with two groups: the National Council of Women and the International Council of Women.

A formal portrait of May Wright Sewall taken by the Indianapolis photography studio Marceau & Power, circa 1880.

The Girls' Classical School in Indianapolis opened in September 1882 on the southeast corner of Pennsylvania and Saint Joseph Streets in the former Saint Anna's school, an Episcopalian girls' institution of learning.

HOME OF WASHINGTON, MOUNT VERNON, VA.

LUKE C. DILLON, PHOTOGRAPHER,
WASHINGTON, D. C.

OFFICE, 933 PENN. AVENUE
PULLMAN'S GALLERY.

May Wright Sewall (left) and her husband Theodore Sewall (right) chaperoned nine students from the Girls'
Classical School on a trip to Washington, D.C. Here the group poses for the camera in front of Mount
Vernon, the home of George Washington.

The original Propylaeum building in Indianapolis was located on the south side of North Street, between Meridian and Pennsylvania Streets.

Members of the Indianapolis Woman's Club gather for the group's last meeting at the original Propylaeum on North Street in Indianapolis on 16 March 1923.

The Art Association of Indianapolis selected the Talbott property (also known as the Tinker House) at Sixteenth and Pennsylvania Streets to become the first home of the John Herron Art Institute.

Lafayette's Helen Gougar proved to be both a friend and opponent of May Wright Sewall through the years.

America's leading women's rights supporters gathered in Washington, D.C. from 25 March to 1 April 1888 for the first Internatinal Council of Women. The group included May Wright Sewall (second row, second from right), Elizabeth Cady Stanton (first row, fourth from right), Susan B. Anthony (first row, third from left), Frances E. Willard (second row, fourth from left), and Zerelda Wallace (first row, second from left).

Chapter 4

THE COUNCIL IDEA

Throughout her active life working for numerous causes, May Wright Sewall received numerous expressions of appreciation for her efforts on behalf of women everywhere. Nothing, however, matched the reception she received in Prague during a visit she made there in 1916. When her train from Berlin pulled into the Prague train station, she was astonished to see a great crowd assembled to greet her. As May stepped from the train, representatives from the city government presented her with an elaborately illuminated manuscript in the Czech language, and May was whisked away to the community's council chambers to address the city. The crowds were so great at the hall that the head of the city government could not make his way through to give his welcoming speech. "It was," she later said of the event, "the most beautiful, the sweetest and the most romantic experience of my life."[1]

The Indiana educator and suffragist achieved her international fame through her pioneering efforts on behalf of the "council idea," which would bring together women from around the world. To May, the essence of her idea was harmony. She aimed to bring "together unlike people committed to different interests in order that they may demonstrate to one another how far their resemblances transcend their differences and to what degree they are capable of uniting in the accomplishment of a common unselfish purpose."[2] What was needed, she believed, was to show club women—who were for the most part only interested in women of their own class—that although they had different social, religious, and political interests, they "were equally related to larger interests; that indeed the likenesses existing among the most different classes of women were larger than the differences among the same classes." May's idea grew into a plan for a

National Council of Women for the United States as well as countries throughout the world, and eventually a permanent International Council of Women composed of national councils.[3] Using her genius for organizing, May, who served as president of the International Council of Women from 1899 to 1904, won for herself the distinction of leader of an "'eternal feminine' following of 5,000,000 in eleven countries."[4]

The grand plans for an international confederacy of women received its initial impetus from the work of May's two old suffragette allies Susan B. Anthony and Elizabeth Cady Stanton. In 1882 Stanton visited England and France and, after discussions with "distinguished publicists and reformers of different countries," decided that an international woman suffrage association should be organized. During the next year Stanton, joined by Anthony, discussed the idea with suffragists in Great Britain. At a reception held in their honor in November before the two feminist pioneers returned home to America, Stanton and Anthony presented their idea to friends of woman's suffrage gathered at the reception and in return received a favorable response. Those gathered for the event passed a resolution stating that the "time has come when women all over the world should unite in the just demand for their political enfranchisement," and went on to appoint a committee of correspondence preparatory to forming an International Woman Suffrage Association. A committee comprising forty-one members representing men and women from the United States, England, Ireland, Scotland, and France was created to plan for such an association, but the group never convened.[5]

The movement for an international suffrage association languished for four years with only a few letters of "mutual encouragement" passed back and forth across the Atlantic Ocean.[6] All that changed at the National Woman Suffrage Association's nineteenth annual convention in 1887 where plans were made to celebrate the fortieth anniversary of the 1848 Seneca Falls meeting by holding an International Council of Women in Washington, D.C., from 25 March to 1 April 1888. At the NWSA convention, however, the ideas of pioneer suffragists such as Stanton and Anthony clashed with the views of a younger generation of women represented in part by May. "Many of the older women . . . at first desired the proposed international meeting to be limited to the advocacy of equal political rights," she noted. "The younger women, who belonged to women's clubs, to the Association of Collegiate Alumnae and to various other progressive movements in which conservative women and even anti-suffragists were associated with them, wished the plan to be extended to workers along all lines of human progress." Toward that end, she introduced a resolution calling for the convening of an International Council of Women "to which women workers in all lines of social, intellectual, moral or civil progress and reform shall be invited, whether they be advocates of the ballot or opposed to woman suffrage." May's wish for an international meeting open to all women won the day, but Anthony and other older suffragists did manage to modify the resolution to read that the meeting, to be sponsored by the NWSA, would include "all associations of women in the trades, professions and moral reforms, as well as those advocating the political emancipation of women."[7] Anthony in particular had balked at a broad invitation allowing anti-suffragists to attend the gathering, issuing the warning that "those active in great philanthropic enterprises [will] sooner or later realize that so long as women are not acknowledged to be political equals of men, their judgment on public questions will have but little weight."[8]

The formidable task of planning and preparing for the meeting fell to the NWSA's executive committee, but most of the work was put upon the shoulders of Sewall, Anthony, and Rachel Foster Avery. The first task undertaken by this suffragist trio involved the writing of a call inviting women to attend the meeting. In composing the call, the three women had many disagreements, with most of the complaints emanating from May. After receiving one fourteen-page letter of suggestions for the call from her friend in Indiana, Anthony wrote Avery in late April 1887 expressing both her opposition to what she called Sewall's "soliloquy" and her frustration over the executive committee's failure to come to a consensus on the call. "May thinks she had everything all right . . . but none of the rest of us think with her," Anthony said.[9] Just a month later, however, Anthony's irritation at Sewall and her nitpickings on the call had turned to admiration at the Hoosier's dedication. "May is just as full of work every minute as ever—it tires one to see her go—but then she has everything so perfectly systematized . . . that she accomplished everything just as she plans," Anthony wrote Avery. "She is a marvel as to executive ability."[10]

By June 1887 the NWSA executive committee had finally agreed on a call for the international meeting at Albaugh's Opera House in Washington, D.C. But even at the last minute, there were changes. Anthony confided in her diary that when she received the proof for the call for the council she "struck out the paragraph saying 'no one would be committed to suffrage who should attend.' I can't allow any such apologetic invitation as that! There is no need to say anything about it."[11] The committee had high hopes for the gathering, noting that exchanging opinions on the great questions of the day "will rouse women to new thought, will intensify their love of liberty and will give them a realizing sense of the power of combination." Although the call claimed that women throughout the world had been "trammeled by their political subordination," it went on to say discussion at the meeting would not be limited to "questions touching the political rights of women." Toward that end, groups invited to attend would include "literary clubs, art unions, temperance unions, labor leagues, missionary, peace and moral purity societies, charitable, professional, educational and industrial associations."[12]

With the call for the meeting completed, Sewall and Foster, under Anthony's watchful eye, turned their attentions to corresponding with women's organizations. May compiled a list of groups in the United States, while Foster, who had traveled overseas on behalf of the suffrage cause, secured a similar list in foreign countries. In contacting approximately one hundred women's organizations in America, May discovered "a timidity in accepting an invitation from a suffrage society as well as other limitations which gave much new sociological information to the Committee having preparations in charge." From her experience with these different groups, she came to develop in full her council idea, uniting women "on the most democratic basis for the largest interests." May had shared her plans with other suffragists, including Ida Husted Harper. Later, when confusion reigned over who should have the credit for creating both the national and international councils, Harper wrote Sewall the following: "I remember distinctly a long talk I had with you in the library of your home in Indianapolis in 1887. You then outlined to me in full detail the plan of a National and an International Council of Women, which should be formed at the International Council that was to meet in Washington in March, 1888, and you said they would far exceed in scope any organi-zation of women in existence."[13]

The effort put forth by Sewall, Avery, and Anthony bore fruit. When Anthony opened the meeting in March 1888 forty-nine delegates were on hand representing England, France, Denmark, Norway, Finland, India, Canada, and the United States. Also, fifty-three different national or-ganizations of women were represented. When the council opened on the morning of 25 March, delegates filed into an auditorium "fragrant with evergreens and flowers, brilliant with rich furniture, [and] crowded with distinguished women."[14] Although speakers discussed such topics as education, temperance, legal and political conditions, and professions, the highlight of the convocation came when May laid out the details of her council idea. On the afternoon of 24 March in the Red Parlor of the Riggs House, Sewall, at the request of chairman Anthony, briefly discussed her idea of forming two permanent organizations, national and international, that "should make possible at regular intervals representative meetings of the same inclusive character." May asked the group to appoint a committee to consider the question, and a fifteen-member body—including Sewall, Avery, Clara Barton, and Frances Willard—met and wrote a constitution embodying the ideas outlined by Sewall. The constitution for the National Council of Women of the United States, which delegates to the meeting approved on 31 March, stated the following:

We, women of the United States, sincerely believing that the best good of our homes and nation will be advanced by our own greater unity of thought, sympathy, and purpose, and that an organized movement of women will best conserve the highest good of the family and the state, do hereby band ourselves together in a confederation of workers committed to the overthrow of all forms of ignorance and injustice, and to the application of the Golden Rule to society, custom and law.

This council is organized in the interest of no one propaganda, and has no power over its auxiliaries beyond that of suggestion and sympathy; therefore, no society voting to become auxiliary to this Council, shall there-by render itself liable to be interfered with in respect to its complete organic unity, independence, or methods of work, or be committed to any principle or method of any other society or to any utterance or act of the Council itself, beyond compliance with the terms of this Constitution.[15]

In addition, the delegates passed a constitution for an International Council of Women, a document similar in form to the one approved for the National Council. Officers for the National Council included Willard as president and Sewall as corresponding secretary, while Millicent Garrett Fawcett was appointed, in absentia, as president of the International Council. Willard and Sewall agreed that the work of the National Council should at first concentrate on ensuring a National Council's formation in another country. Toward that end, May went to Europe in the summer of 1889 to meet with Fawcett and to discuss her council idea at an International Congress of Women in Paris. Although Fawcett had earlier indicated her willingness to organize a council in Great Britain (she wrote in 1884 that England and America "should be leading the way in this question of the representation of women"), she refused to follow through on the work. One historian of the women's movement perceived a "clash of temperaments" between the American and British suffragists. According to May, Fawcett gave several reasons for her refusal to assume the presidency and organize a council in England, including her busy schedule and the time not yet being "ripe" for federating the country's existing women's organizations. Sewall also quoted Fawcett as saying it was "quite impossible that English and American women should have anything in common, the conditions of their lives and the purposes of their respective societies being so different."[16]

Encountering resistance in England, May had better luck in Paris, where she outlined her council idea to a foreign audience for the first time. In her remarks to the exposition, she encouraged French women to organize their own council. The object of such a group, May said, would be to bring all women's organizations into a federation and provide for regular triennial meetings. "In these meetings," she told the crowd, "every cause or object represented by the National organizations which have joined the federation will be discussed by its advocates, and its progress will be officially report-ed." The national council itself, she continued, would not promote any one reform or give preference to any cause. The Indiana reformer outlined five goals for the triennial meetings:

> First: They will make an opportunity for women whose work is along different lines, to become personally acquainted with the purposes and the management of organizations in which they have no part and from which they have hitherto held aloof.
>
> Second: It is anticipated that out of acquaintance will spring reciprocal sympathy. Women will learn that the different lines along which they work are, however different, after all con-vergent, and destined to meet in that improved state of human society which all desire.
>
> Third: We see that this National council will prove, or rather, that it will illustrate, the correlation of the spiritual forces of society.
>
> Fourth: This illustration of the correlation of the spiritual forces of society cannot fail to exert a great and ultimately commanding influence upon public opinion in our country.
>
> Fifth: In these meetings will convene not the mere repre-sentative of states, of geographical territory, but in them will meet the representatives of great humanitarian enterprises, of spiritual aspirations, of political and social reforms, or moral and religious movements.[17]

After the Paris congress, May continued to evangelize on behalf of the council idea in Switzerland, giving talks at "drawing-room meetings" in

Geneva and Zurich and distributing to all who would take it a call for local women's groups having the same objectives to form national societies that could then subsequently become eligible for membership in the National Council of Women (the national groups could then join the International Council of Women). These new organizations might then have the power, May theorized, to seek such reforms as placing women on local school boards and panels overseeing benevolent and public institutions; gaining admission to press associations, medical societies, and religious organizations; and asking for physical and industrial training for female students in public schools. "It will be readily seen," May said, "that greatly added force will come from any such movement, whether local, state or national, when it is backed by the united societies of the locality, state or nation, and that, with a small expenditure of time and money, all these societies . . . may also do an immense work for womanhood at large along the lines on which all can agree to unite in sympathy, influence, and effort."[18]

Her dream of a national confederation of local and state clubs did come true for May, but not in the manner in which she had envisioned. In January 1889 at the regular business meeting of Sorosis, usually considered the first organized woman's club in America, Jennie Cunningham Croly proposed that the organization celebrate its upcoming twenty-first anniversary by sponsoring a convention of clubs from around the country. Delegates meeting at Madison Square Garden in New York two months later laid the foundation for a new organization: the General Federation of Women's Clubs. Ella Dietz Clymer, Sorosis president, predicted that the GFWC would "stand related to clubs throughout this land, and, eventually throughout the world, as a great mother to her children—inspiring and controlling by the forces of wisdom and love."[19]

May attended the meeting as a delegate and served on a committee whose job it was to draft a constitution for the new organization. She also worked hard to recruit clubs in Indiana, Ohio, and Kentucky to join the GFWC, sending personal letters to thirty-six clubs in the three states, plus an additional four in Minnesota and the Dakotas. In April 1890 delegates ratified the GFWC's constitution and elected two of the constitution's five authors as its top officials—Charlotte Brown as president and May as vice president. All seemed to be going according to May's wishes, but the group proved to be more independent than she had bargained for. The federation, which considered itself "a sovereign and international body," declined to join the National Council of Women.[20]

In spite of her setback with the GFWC, May continued with her efforts on behalf of her cherished council idea. When the National Council of Women held its first triennial meeting from 22 to 26 February 1891, the organization's membership included such groups as the National Woman Suffrage Association, the National Woman's Christian Temperance Union, the Woman's National Press Association, the National Women's Relief Society, the Young Ladies National Mutual Improvement Association, and the National Free Baptist Woman's Missionary Society. During its meeting, the council approved a bold set of resolutions including calling on the Methodist Episcopal Church to admit women to its general conference; urging the National Divorce Reform League to place women on its board; appointing a committee to suggest a business costume for women to "meet the demands of health, comfort and good taste"; approving the movement against killing birds for use in clothing ornamentation; and asking the federal government to pay its employees equal pay for equal work.[21]

One resolution, however, proved to portend great things for both the national and international councils. Noting that the four hundredth anniversary of Columbus's discovery of the New World would be celebrated at a World's Exposition in Chicago in 1893, the National Council, which at that time was the de facto International Council, decided to hold the first meeting of the International Council at Chicago. The exposition seemed to be the perfect place for such a gathering. In addition to appropriating funds for the celebration, the U.S. Congress had also approved an amendment by Illinois representative William Springer to a bill creating the National Commission whose job it would be to coordinate the fair. Springer's amendment established a Board of Lady Managers "to perform such duties as may be prescribed by said Commission." Chicago socialite Bertha H. Palmer was selected to serve as president of the Board of Lady Managers, and she invited the National Council of Women to hold its international meeting at Chicago, promising to make available to the group "the assembly room in the Woman's building, and should that not prove large enough, from our Congress Auxiliary, the magnificent auditorium can be secured for the meetings of the International Council of Women."[22]

To obtain the necessary cooperation from international groups to make the Chicago exposition a success, May, who had taken over for Willard as president of the National Council of Women, once again traveled to Europe to campaign on behalf of her council idea. In 1891 she visited such countries as France, Switzerland, Italy, Belgium, and Germany. In addition to her work overseas, May had been working to convince Charles C. Bonney, president of the World's Congress Auxiliary, which was responsible for sponsoring congresses at the fair to consider "great themes," to adopt the first International Council of Women meeting as one of those official congresses. In her history of the ICW, May noted it took "much correspondence and several interviews" before Bonney agreed to the proposition, with the understanding that the meeting's scope should be "enlarged to the greatest possible extent," and it should take the name the World's Congress of Representative Women. Bonney appointed May to chair the organizing committee for the women's congress, which would be held the week of 15 May 1893.[23]

Working once again with Avery, who had been named by Bonney to act as corresponding secretary for the women's congress organizing committee, May continued to beat the drum for the international council with women in Europe. Meanwhile, Avery worked to compile lists of national organizations of women that existed in all countries, and to secure their participation in the upcoming congress. With Sewall's return to America in September 1892, thousands of copies of a preliminary address outlining the purpose of the World's Congress of Representative Women were issued. The address promised that at the congress "every living question pertaining to the education or the employment of women may be discussed." The sessions at the congress, the address continued, would include "the women's view upon every issue affecting humanity—upon the home, the church, the state, and her own function in these institutions." Between September 1892 and May 1893, Sewall and Avery's organizing committee distributed 7,198 letters and another 55,000 printed documents to women in such countries as Austria, Holland, Portugal, Spain, Poland, Mexico, Argentina, Peru, Brazil, Guatemala, China, Japan, Iceland, New Zealand, India, Syria, Turkey, New South Wales, Siam, Samoa, and the Sandwich Islands. Impressed by these efforts, Anthony wrote Sewall: "The suffrage work has missed you, oh, so much, still I would not have had you do differently. I glory in Rachel's and your work this year beyond words."[24]

Her grand hopes for the women's congress and her devotion to the two new women's councils, however, placed May at odds with two influential Chicago women: Palmer, president of the Board of Lady Managers at the fair and president of the woman's branch of the World's Congress Auxiliary, and Ellen Henrotin, vice president of the auxiliary's woman's branch. Both Palmer and Henrotin not only viewed Sewall as a "radical feminist," but also they saw her as using the congress as a way to promote the two councils she championed. Palmer and Henrotin's suspicions about May were heightened in September 1892 when they learned of a letter she had sent to Mary Logan, a leader of the Woman's Relief Corps. In the letter, printed on National Council stationery, May informed Logan that it was "a most auspicious time for a National Organization to enter the Council," as the National Council had "really been given charge of the World's Congress." Because Logan was a woman "accustomed to considering large views, and entertaining large ideas," May said it would be unnecessary for her to "present arguments for bringing the Relief Corps into the Council. Such arguments will present themselves to your mind more rapidly and more clearly than I could present them to you."[25]

As officers of the congress auxiliary, Palmer and Henrotin greatly resented May's claim that the National Council of Women was running the congress, and also feared that women's organizations and clubs might believe they had to join the national council if they wanted to participate in the congress. Palmer even went so far as to consult Bonney about the matter, telling Henrotin of the following conversation with him: "I said I was afraid that some of our power might have been given away, as Mrs.

Sewall had not consulted or reported to me, and he said, 'Certainly not, you stand at the head.'" Emboldened by Bonney's support, Palmer wrote May warning the suffragist that her actions in trying to usurp control of the congress "make no new allies, and no new friends. Your friends will of course stand by you, but those who are doubtful will hold aloof." Palmer also told May that from then on she was to forward all official letters and replies to her in Chicago.[26]

The struggle for control of the World's Congress of Representative Women took its toll on May, who at one point threatened to resign. The storm passed, however, thanks in no little part to the soothing words offered by Sewall's friend and fellow suffragist Avery. Writing to Sewall from her home in Philadelphia, Avery reiterated her love for May and her faith in her motives. She went on to write: "It is *because* I feel so well assured of our mutual confidence that I dare to say that . . . I would willingly sacrifice for you and for myself everything except self-respect rather than retire from the positions which we voluntarily entered upon. *Nothing* could repay either of us should we allow any personal feeling to make us leave this Congress in the hands of the people to whom we know its conduct would fall were we to resign. *Nothing* would make up to us in our whole after-lives for the knowledge that this Congress, instead of being what we could have made it, was a failure."[27]

Buoyed by Avery's strong support, May stayed on in her position and was able to witness, when the congress convened in May, the coming together of 126 women's organizations from such countries as the United States, Canada, Great Britain, Denmark, Belgium, Finland, Italy, Norway, France, Germany, Sweden, and Switzerland. During the week, eighty-one sessions were held featuring 333 speakers, with as many as eighteen sessions held at one time in different halls. Clarence Young, secretary of the World's Congress Auxiliary, estimated total attendance for the week at approximately one hundred and fifty thousand, and police who provided security for the congress "testified that often hundreds of people were sent away long before the hour for opening a meeting arrived."[28]

The behind-the-scenes battles between Sewall, Palmer, and Henrotin seemed forgotten as the congress received glowing reviews, including praise from the *New York Times*, which termed the meeting as "one of the most brilliant gatherings of women ever assembled." But controversy continued to plague May as the congress ended, this time from a familiar source: her old Hoosier adversary, Helen Gougar. On 20 May 1893 newspapers from throughout the country reported Gougar's claim that Sewall had conspired to keep her from being allowed to speak at the congress and ordered her name stricken from the meeting's official program. "The idea of anybody trying to hold a congress of representative women and ignoring Helen Gougar! Wow!" exclaimed one correspondent. "I don't want to pose as a disturber," Gougar was quoted by the *Philadelphia Press*, "but I had to do something to protect myself. It seems that the order was issued on Mrs. May Wright Sewall's responsibility. Mrs. Sewall and I have been personal enemies for some time." Before leaving Chicago on a speaking tour in the west, May denied issuing any such order. Her claim was backed by Henrotin, who wrote a letter stating that Gougar had not been blackballed by congress officials.[29]

Lost in the hoopla and controversy of the World's Congress of Representative Women were the first tentative steps toward making the International Council of Women a viable organization. At the Chicago gathering, the ICW met and heard reports about the possible formation of national councils in Canada, France, Finland, and other Scandinavian countries. More important, the ICW elected as its new president Lady Aberdeen, a Scottish aristocrat and wife of the governor general of Canada. Although caught off guard by the honor, Aberdeen accepted the post; one she would hold almost continuously until 1936. She worked hard to form a national council in Canada. "It was from experience in the Canadian Council," said Aberdeen, "and in watching its development through a chain of local councils between the Atlantic and Pacific, that I began to understand this idea of bringing together diverse people to work for common causes." After taking office, Aberdeen sent her private secretary, Teresa Wilson, who spoke French and German, to Europe to aid in creating national councils. From 1893 to the ICW's 1899 quinquennial congress in England, national councils were also formed in Germany, Great Britain, Sweden, Australia, Denmark, and the Netherlands.[30]

With the ICW firmly established as a viable organization, May next turned her attention toward an issue that came to dominate her life: international peace. For May, the desire of women for peace came from their view of war as "a menace to the whole spirit of the home, a menace to the children born and reared within the home." The only war to which a woman could give "her heart is that war whose object it is to slay war and establish peace."[31] At first, May helped to convince the National Council of Women to work on behalf of peace. "Originally," she noted, "it was the unwritten law of the National Council that no propaganda should be adopted by it until after it had been endorsed by the unanimous vote of its Committee." Although the matter was discussed at the National Council's executive sessions in 1893 and 1894, it wasn't until the group's second triennial meeting in Washington on 2 March 1895 that the council approved a resolution committing the group to the active promotion of peace and to supporting the efforts of Czar Nicholas II of Russia, who had called for a conference at The Hague to establish a panel for international arbitration. "It is the opinion of this body," the NCW resolution stated, "that a permanent National Board of Peace and Arbitration should be added to our Government, and we respectfully suggest that a Peace Commission composed of men and women shall be appointed or otherwise provided to confer with the governments of other Nations upon the subject of establishing an International Court of Arbitration." In addition to approving the peace resolution, the National Council also created a standing committee on social peace and international arbitration and, from 1899 to 1905, supported peace meetings throughout the country. These meetings, held each 18 May, grew over the years from 74 in number in 1899 to 422 by 1902.[32]

May's work on behalf of international peace with the National Council paved the way for similar efforts with the ICW. At the organization's second quinquennial meeting in London in 1899—a meeting at which May became the ICW's president—representatives from ten national councils of women gathered and made the "far-reaching decision" to pledge the ICW's support on the arbitration of international disputes. Both the American and Canadian representatives presented similar resolutions on the subject, and the ICW finally adopted a measure pledging to "take steps in every country to further and advance by every means in their power the movement towards International Arbitration." (This resolution was reconfirmed by the organization at its 1904 meeting in Berlin and its 1909 gathering in Toronto.) The group also formed a standing committee on peace and international arbitration with May as its chairman. The resolution, she noted, committed the ICW to peace "as its first, and for five years its only propaganda," with the standing committee working to promote the idea.[33] Through its approval of the peace measure, the ICW, according to May, would work for the following:

> . . . not for the abatement of war, but for its extinction; not to the limitation of armaments but the remanding of the war ships into the museums of history, where it will require as much patience and skill to reconstruct their forms and rehabilitate them as it now requires scientific skill to reproduce the form of the mastodon.
>
> Our result, our ultimate object, is the cessation of all warfare by the extinction of all competition, by the supplanting of competition by co-operation, by the displacement of hate, all international hate and international envy, by international affection. That is indeed no sentimental ground, . . . it had its origin in our creation, born out of the heart of God. This humanity, which the conflict of its development upon this plane has divided into so many races, but which its evolution into the likeness of its father shall unite.[34]

To secure such lofty goals, the ICW actively promoted peace through its yearly executive meetings, which were held in the capitals of the different countries represented in the organization, and also agitated on the issue at a number of international expositions. May used the bully pulpit of the ICW presidency as a way to clamor for such reforms as the elimination of nationalism from school textbooks. The council, May noted, asked each of its affiliated national councils to instruct their committees on peace and arbitration to conduct a "rigid examination of all textbooks on the history of their own country which are being studied in its schools. This is to be done with a view to ascertaining to what degree the relative importance of war in the development of a country and the relative glory of military achievement are exaggerated in such textbooks." In the case of the United States, May encouraged the adoption of textbooks that emphasized how industry developed in the country through "successive tides of immigration." To her way of thinking, it seemed futile "for us to meet in peace congresses and discuss with some degree of respect the great nations, and do nothing to abate the mutual ignorance and consequent dislike, not to say hatred, of the representatives of different races in the different cities in which we live." May also encouraged mothers throughout the world to remove from their children's nursery toys that "bring into a child's mind the thought of military pomp and show, of warfare, with its contentions and its glories."[35]

Even after her term as ICW president ended in 1904, May continued to campaign on behalf of peace through her chairmanship of the council's standing committee on peace and arbitration. She became a familiar presence at national and international peace conferences, always ready to address the faithful on this important issue. May's promotion of peace continued unabated with the outbreak of World War I in 1914. On a visit to Italy in June 1914 she received a telegraph informing her that she had been appointed by Charles C. Moore president of the Panama-Pacific International Exposition in San Francisco, to organize an international conference of women workers for the promotion of cooperative internationalism. Before May could begin work on the conference, war in Europe broke out, "temporarily paralyzing the public mind," she noted, and "rendering uncertain" the San Francisco exposition. "While many distinguished advocates of Peace felt that work for its establishment was inevitably suspended by the war—to me the war seemed a proclamation to the women of the world that some action by them which would assert the solidarity of womanhood was imperative," she said.[36]

Undisturbed by the bloody conflict raging in Europe, May set out to make the conference a success, enlisting for her organizing committee such notable women as Jane Addams, Carrie Chapman Catt, Anna Garlin Spencer, Ida Husted Harper, and Lucia Ames Mead (also joining the

committee were Hoosier friends Harriet Noble and Grace Julian Clarke).
Although Addams gave little help to the group's efforts because of her
election as chairman of the Women's Peace party, other members of the
committee more than made up the slack, addressing meetings in Massachusetts, New Hampshire, New York, Maryland, Pennsylvania, Ohio,
Indiana, Illinois, Minnesota, Louisiana, Mississippi, Alabama, Oregon,
Washington, and California. In addition, the committee distributed more
than 200,000 page of literature on the conference to women's clubs,
teachers' institutes, parents' associations, patriotic societies, Sunday schools,
Chautauqua assemblies, and other gatherings. May herself sent personal
letters to international groups and received in response to her correspondence and published announcements about the conference approximately 2,700 responses.[37]

May's genius for organization, and the work of her committee, paid off
when the International Conference of Women Workers to Promote
International Peace opened in San Francisco in July 1915. The conference
drew approximately 500 delegates representing the United States and
eleven other countries. In addition to hearing numerous speakers pro-
moting peace, including an address by William Jennings Bryan, who had
resigned his post as secretary of state under President Woodrow Wilson
before the conference opened, delegates passed a number of resolutions
regarding peace. The resolutions included protests against military drill
in schools, using public funds to glorify war, and the signing of secret
treaties between governments. Women at the conference went on to
demand the creation of an international legislative body, international
court, and international police; called on nations to agree to a general
disarmament; sought full political rights for women nationally and
internationally; and urged that neutral nations, which at that time included
the United States, create a conference of such countries to mediate among
the warring powers until peace could be restored.[38]

Conferences and resolutions were well and good, but May believed in
taking a more direct approach to achieve her dreams of international
harmony. In November 1915 she received a telegram that placed her
squarely in the middle of a fantastic venture to stop the bloodshed in

Europe: the Ford Peace Trip. The telegram was from American automotive magnate Henry Ford, who had a plan that he believed would "put a stop to the silly killings going on abroad" and get "the boys out of the trenches by Christmas."[39] Ford asked May to join him and other like-minded people in an expedition to Europe aboard a chartered Danish ocean liner, the *Oscar II*, which sailed from Hoboken, New Jersey, on 4 December. May accepted Ford's offer and became one of sixty peace delegates who, she believed, were not "hair-brained lunatics," as many in the press intimated, but instead a "company of clear-headed but simple-hearted men and women" working together to achieve a common goal: peace.[40] May's high hopes for the expedition, however, would be put to a stern test by not only the actions of the members of the press on board, but also by the behavior of her fellow delegates.

Chapter 5

THE PEACE TRIP

In the early afternoon of 4 December 1915, a crowd estimated at anywhere from three thousand to fifteen thousand braved the brisk weather at a pier in Hoboken, New Jersey, in order to witness the sailing of the Scandinavian-American liner *Oscar II*, which was set for a scheduled ten-day trip through hostile waters to Christiania (today Oslo), Norway. Amid scenes called by the *Philadelphia North American* "so remarkably extravagant as to be almost beyond belief," the crowd sang and cheered as a band on shore and on the ship played such stirring tunes as "I Didn't Raise My Boy to Be a Soldier" and "Onward, Christian Soldiers." The biggest cheers were reserved for the sponsor of this unusual adventure: industrialist Henry Ford, who the previous August had declared his willingness to devote his fortune in order to ensure peace. Unable to discover any "honourable reasons" for the war, Ford believed, he said later, that some nations "were anxious for peace and would welcome a demonstration for peace." Under the encouragement of Rosika Schwimmer, a Hungarian author, lecturer, and peace advocate, Ford had secured passage on the liner for approximately sixty delegates in an attempt to halt the war now raging in Europe through the establishment of a neutral commission whose job it would be to offer continuous mediation among the belligerent nations.[1]

May was one of the more than one hundred people, including such notables as Thomas Edison, Jane Addams, William Howard Taft, and William Jennings Bryan, to receive invitations from Ford to join him on the voyage. The first word of the trip came to May on 24 November when she received a telegram from Ford, followed three days later by a letter in which the automotive maker spelled out in more detail his reasons for asking May to join him and others on the voyage. "From the moment I realized that the world situation demands immediate action, if we do not want the war fire to spread any further," Ford wrote, "I joined those international forces which are working toward ending this unparalleled catastrophe." Saying it was his "human duty" to work for peace, Ford went on to proclaim that the world looked to America "to lead in ideals. The greatest mission ever before a nation is ours." The itinerary outlined by Ford included stops in Norway, Sweden, and Denmark before the delegation's eventual destination, the Hague in the Netherlands. Along the way, the peace expedition hoped to entice ten citizens from each country to join its cause.[2]

Of course, Ford, as a leader in the business world, did not handle the details of what came to be known as the Ford Peace Ship. That responsibility fell mainly to Schwimmer and Louis P. Lochner, a writer and former student activist. Although May's work with the National Council of Women and International Council of Women had won her worldwide fame, her inclusion on the trip more than likely came about through her acquaintanceship with Schwimmer, who had been the delegate from Hungary at the IWC's meeting at the Hague in April 1915. That November, Schwimmer, through the good graces of a *Detroit News* reporter, had an interview with Ford at his estate near Detroit. Lochner also had scheduled a meeting with Ford that day, and the two peace advocates convinced Ford to support the idea of continuous mediation. The auto magnate agreed to join Schwimmer in New York to work out details for the plan. In New York Ford met with Schwimmer, Lochner, Addams, and others about sending a mediating commission to Europe. When Lochner joked about sending the delegates abroad on a special ship chartered for the occasion, Ford, who saw the possible positive publicity from such a move, immediately seized on the idea and the Ford Peace Ship was on its way.[3]

Before embarking on his peace crusade, Ford, accompanied by Lochner, met with President Woodrow Wilson to try to convince the chief executive to appoint an official neutral commission, which Ford was willing to back financially. Although noting that he agreed in principle with the idea of continuous mediation, Wilson skillfully avoided endorsing Ford's proposal.

In an attempt to force the president's hand, Ford offered what appeared to be an ultimatum: the next morning Ford would announce to the press that he had secured a ship for a peace delegation. "If you can't act," Ford told Wilson, "I will." The president refused to waver in his determination to avoid officially endorsing Ford's action, ending the meeting. Ford's assessment of the president was blunt, telling Lochner: "He's a small man." Even without Wilson's endorsement, Ford was confident of the trip's success, telling newspapermen in New York the next day that he had chartered a ship and planned on trying to "get the boys out of the trenches before Christmas." Accompanying him, he added, would be a group of the "biggest and most influential peace advocates in the country. The ship would also be armed with "the longest gun in the world—the Marconi [radio]," said Ford, which could "let the world know that we are bound for peace."[4]

Press reaction to Ford's announcement was, at best, mixed. Some of the media gave the automobile tycoon high marks for good intentions, but most were skeptical about Ford's chances of accomplishing his mission. The *New York Evening Post* boldly predicted that the automaker's plan would "be acclaimed by thoughtful hundreds of thousands the world over as a bit of American idealism in an hour when the rest of the world has gone mad over war and war-preparedness." Other newspapers were unstinting in their scorn, calling the mission "one of the cruelest jokes of the century" and an "impossible effort to establish an inopportune peace." With its tongue planted firmly in check, the *Boston Traveler* concluded: "It is not Mr. Ford's purpose to make peace: he will assemble it."[5]

When the *Oscar II* steamed away from the pier on 4 December it had onboard delegates termed as "negligible" in standing by some observers. Although numerous politicians and such respected names as Edison and Bryan had refused to join Ford's peace venture, the group included a respectable number with solid reputations, not only May, but magazine publisher S. S. McClure, Rev. Jenkin Lloyd Jones, and Judge Ben Lindsey. Also on board were approximately twenty-five students, representing institutions as diverse as Vassar, Princeton University, Purdue University, the University of Texas, and the University of California at Berkeley; fifty members of the press, including reporters from United Press, Associated Press, and the International News Service; and twenty-five members of Ford's staff. In assessing her fellow delegates for her friends back home in Indiana, May acknowledged that no one in the party had an "exalted position; not one bearing the stamp of worldwide recognition." She added, however, that none of the delegates were "hair-brained lunatics bent on a fool's errand—but rather a company of clear-headed but simple-hearted men and women, with no illusions in regard to ourselves but with the faith that *any one* of us, much more *all of us with* God, constitutes a majority in that council where each next stop along the path of human progress is determined." Through their work, May said the delegates hoped to accomplish three goals: to secure the public's attention, diverting it from war to peace; to stimulate other private initiatives and encourage workers for peace in every country; and confirm on all those involved their resolution to work for a permanent peace.[6]

Once at sea, the delegates attempted to establish a regular routine. Each day at 11:00 A.M., said May, the student group met to learn more about the "principles involved in this trip." Each session opened with a talk by one of the delegates on a subject in which they were regarded as an expert. The delegates themselves listened to similar speakers each day at 4:00 P.M. and 8:30 P.M., becoming better acquainted with one another through such gatherings, she noted. May's optimism and work on behalf of peace impressed other delegates. One of them, John D. Barry, an essayist, poet, and critic, reflected that in spite of May's age she proved to be one of the "most useful members of the party, keen, and quick of mind, bubbling over with information and observation, humorous, kindly and above all human."[7]

For her talk before the student group, May discussed her work with the International Council of Women, and also touched on the war's effect on that organization. Noting that every ship could withstand a calm sea, May added that the real test of a ship "is what it can do in a storm." Many international organizations, including the IWC, were "shattered by the catastrophe" of the war, she said. But in every country there were women who felt as May did, namely that if "we have been weak in our demands for international solidarity before this, the war was a bugle call awakening us to our duty." Although women as a group were often charged with being subject to their emotions, May said there was no shame in such a fact as an intellect without emotion would be paralyzed. The key, she told the students, came in harnessing these emotional powers in a way that would help lead nations away from war and to peace.[8]

In addition to learning more about each other through meetings and conversation, those on board also kept abreast of events through the ship's official daily newspaper, the *Argosy*, which printed news, poems, humorous pieces, and more serious fare, including a contribution from May on the woman's movement in America. The newspaper even offered a song for the delegates, to be sung to the tune of "Tipperary." The song went:

> Our peace ship party started with a send off at the pier,
> We don't know where we're going—but we're mighty glad we're here,
> It's a seasick sort of voyage, over miles of ocean spray
> But we put our trust in Henry and with faith and hope we say:
> It's a long way to Copenhagen
> It's a long way to sail,
> It's a long way to Copenhagen,
> But we'll get there, never fail.
> Good bye dear old Broadway,
> Farewell Herald Square
> It's a long, long way to Copenhagen,
> But peace waits right there.[9]

As for the ship's most famous passenger, Ford, called by May "the Captain of our Peace Mission," he became a familiar presence to most of the group. Although he kept away from the delegate's assemblies, he did make himself available to the reporters for interviews early in the voyage until a cold forced him to keep mainly to his cabin. Even when ensconced in his cabin, Ford remained, said May, the center of attention of "those of his guests who realize that his own character must inevitably be as unique as the company he has assembled and the mission that he is conducting."

To May, the only natural explanation for Ford's "inspired undertaking" was that he was responding to the "call of the Lord." In examining the businessman's face, May perceived that he was endowed with "the seeing eye, that can discern times and seasons; with the hearing ear that can be penetrated by the still small voice; and with the open mind that can receive its message." From Ford's visage she also saw "a radiant serenity which implies satisfaction in his response to the call."[10]

Ford's goodwill to all on the voyage did have an effect on the ship's passengers, including some cynical newspapermen. One of the members of the media, Florence Lattimore of *Survey* magazine, later related that another reporter confided to her that his employers had told him to produce satirical articles about the trip, but after seeing Ford's face he could not bring himself to follow their dictates. Still another newsman told Lattimore: "I came to make fun of the whole thing, but my editor is going to have the surprise of his life. I tell you I believe in Henry Ford and I'm going to say so even if I lose my job for it."[11] Other reporters, however, were unconvinced by their host's goodwill, treating the entire voyage with derision. A London newspaperman, traveling steerage, even went as far to send a fanciful story about Ford being held prisoner in his cabin, chained to his bed by his staff. But when the *Oscar II*'s captain, J. W. Hempel, who reviewed all messages sent from the ship, took some of the more scurrilous dispatches to Ford, he responded magnanimously, telling Hempel: "Let them send anything they please. I want the boys to feel perfectly at home while they are with me. They are my guests. I wouldn't for the world censor them."[12]

The free flow of information, both accurate and inaccurate, from the ship caused problems for the expedition, as any disagreements among the delegates became fodder for sensational reports. Legend has it that a delegate became so upset about a report from Hoosier Elmer Davis, covering the voyage for the *New York Times*, that he termed the reporter "a snake in the garden of Eden." Davis, who already had helped organize a press club, responded by forming a Snakes in the Garden of Eden Club.[13] The real blowup came, however, when the ship received a wireless report on a speech to Congress by Wilson calling for increased military preparedness. In trying to craft a response to Wilson's speech, sharp disagreements erupted among the delegates, with some calling for immediate disarmament and others arguing that countries should have the necessary arms to defend themselves. McClure was particularly vocal, indicating that while he had worked for international disarmament for years, he could not "impugn the course laid out by the President of the United States." Although the battle ended in a compromise, the incident prompted reporters to wire stories back to their newspapers about "war" and a "mutiny" breaking out on the peace ship. In defending the expedition, Lochner asked reporters to show him "any live community in which there is not healthy disagreement over details." Still, as the ship neared its destination, Lochner did admit that the "closing days of our voyage were not a symphonic poem."[14]

Early in the morning on 18 December the *Oscar II* docked in Christiania, Norway. Physically, May said, Norway gave the delegates a cold welcome, as the weather was reportedly the chilliest in 150 years. "The bleakest east wind I had ever felt in Boston," said May, "was by comparison a May zephyr." The peace expedition also received a cool reception from the Norwegian press, which for the most part favored the Allied cause in the war. The delegates were formally welcomed to the Scandinavian country at an afternoon reception sponsored by the Women's International Peace League, followed by a public meeting at the University of Christiania. With the delegates, including Ford, safely ensconced in the city's Grand Hotel, May, scheduled to speak at a student meeting, had become convinced that to save herself from being frozen to death she must buy a fur-lined cloak, which she accomplished with the help of two friends. She persuaded a local merchant to give her the 10 percent discount that all of his regular native customers received, but which never before had been given to a foreigner. May's Norwegian friends, made through her work with the International Council of Women, also sent over a housekeeper to "fit my coat and make whatever changes were necessary."[15]

The peace expedition barely had time to settle into its new surroundings when it received a shocking blow: Ford had decided to go home. Unable to shake the cold he had caught onboard ship, and encouraged to do so by his staff, Ford had decided to leave in time to catch a ship bound for America. According to Lochner, who had been "deeply shocked" by Ford's appearance when he visited in his hotel room, the automaker told him: "Guess I had better go home to mother [his wife Clara]. You've got this thing started now and can get along without me." Lochner attempted to convince Ford to stay with the expedition, but failed. On 23 December, as the delegates prepared to leave Norway by train for Stockholm, Sweden, Ford slipped out of his hotel and took another train to Bergen, Norway. Most of the delegates, including May, believed that Ford had boarded their train, which had been delayed by snow-covered tracks and a frozen engine, to make the frigid journey to Stockholm.[16]

The trip proved to be an uncomfortable one for many of the delegates, as the snow and cold conspired to make what would have been a twelve-hour journey into a twenty-two-hour nightmare. Trapped in unheated compartments with no provisions for food and without sleeping cars, some of the delegates attempted to cheer themselves by singing, including a spirited rendition of "Sweet Adeline" by Rev. Theolopsis Montgomery. During the long and exhausting train ride, May lost some respect for her fellow delegates. "Many people," she said, "were unable to talk of anything but the deprivations that they were experiencing, the cold, thirst, hunger and general discomfort." She reflected that within a few hundred miles of the train there were "thousands upon thousands of soldiers to whom the worst discomfort that this journey brought would be an enviable luxury."[17]

Although May indicated the weather was so cold that it "was beyond language to describe," she managed, as the train sped on to its destination, to comfort herself by observing the surrounding countryside. The scenery the train passed through, she noted, was "so varied, so wild and beautiful that the physical discomfort was quite lost in the joy of it." As day turned to night, a bright moon lit the landscape, making the glorious forests visible to her. The moonlight also illuminated another feature: people gathered by the train tracks. "Until long past midnight in that awful cold," said May, "people came through drifting snows, facing ice-laden winds, just to see the train that was bearing the Ford Expedition to Stockholm."[18]

Arriving in Stockholm early in the morning on 24 December, the delegates were shocked to discover that Ford had abandoned them. According to May, she and other delegates were eating dinner at the hotel when they received a cable from Ford on board a ship bound for New York. "His doctor says it is imperative he [Ford] should go at once for a long rest," May reported. "Mr. Ford cables us that if it is possible he shall return to us to meet us at the Hague." Upon his return to America, Ford told the media he had not deserted and offered no regrets for the peace trip, expressing the belief that "the sentiment we have aroused by making the people think will shorten the war." With Ford's departure, the expedition turned for leadership to a committee consisting of delegates Charles Aked, Mary Fels, Frederick Holt, Ben Huebsch, Jenkin Lloyd Jones, Ben Lindsey, and Lola Maverick Lloyd. In addition, policy matters would be handled by Schwimmer and financial concerns by Ford staff member Gaston Plantiff. [19]

The peace expedition spent a week in Stockholm, developing a regular schedule, according to May. Each morning at 10:00 A.M. the delegates met to discuss the day's activities. From 11:30 A.M. to 1:00 P.M. the group hosted a reception at the hotel open to the public. The delegates had time to themselves until 4:00 P.M., when the expedition hosted a second public reception. In helping to welcome visitors to the receptions, May observed that they seemed to fall into four categories: teachers, feminists, social reformers, and students. "I was particularly interested in the university students," she said, "who, although it was their holiday week, called in great numbers. I was amazed by both the intelligence, and by the lively interest in serious subjects of these young people, whom I was mentally comparing with my young countrymen and countrywomen of student age to the distinct disadvantage of the latter. The teachers of my own country being . . . rather narrow in their interests, rigid in their conservatism and timid in their expression of advance opinions when they chance to hold them, I was hardly less surprised by their prominence and outspokenness among our visitors than by that of the students." In talking to others about the students, she learned that most of them who called on the expedition belonged to Sweden's Socialist party, were poor, and were working their way through school. One Swede told May that in talking to the youngsters she was not "seeing Stockholm of today—but rather intellectual Sweden of the near future."[20]

While in Sweden, May also kept busy by giving speeches, including one to a group of Swedish women. After her speech, one woman told her she had in her possession her portrait and a copy of the first suffrage speech May had ever given. "She told me that this had been among her treasures for the last 20 years," May said. In addition to speeches, she also indulged herself in a bit of diplomacy. After breakfast one day, May was introduced to the private secretary for Ira Nelson Morris, the U.S. minister to Norway. The secretary arranged for a private interview between May and Morris. During the meeting, she told the minister that she was particularly concerned about French misunderstandings about the motives of peace workers in America during the war. "I confessed to him frankly that my sympathies were with France," she said, "and that my most intimate friendships were with French women and men and that I desired above everything to communicate very frankly my interpretation of the Ford Peace Mission as well as my private affection to my French friends and asked if he could transmit a letter from me under the seal of the [U.S.] legation to the American minister at Paris." Although May found Morris "exceedingly kind," he could not fulfill her request, as he had been instructed by his superiors in Washington, D.C., to send no letters from his legation except for those concerning official government business.[21]

The peace expedition needed its own brand of diplomacy to reach its eventual destination, the Hague. Leaving Sweden for Denmark on 30 December, the group discovered that the Danish government had recently passed a law prohibiting foreigners from giving addresses on the war. Working quickly, the delegates were able to discuss their goals at meetings sponsored by private clubs and groups. In order to reach the group's final stop, Holland, the delegates had to travel, via a sealed train, through German territory, a feat accomplished through the intercession of the American minister to Denmark. Once in Holland, the group selected delegates for the Neutral Conference for Continuous Mediation, which would have its headquarters in Stockholm. With this final task completed, the delegates and students could finally return home. On 15 January 1916 the delegates left port aboard the *Rotterdam* for the voyage back to America (the students had left four days earlier on the *Noordam*).[22]

The immediate reaction to the Ford Peace Ship once the delegates returned was that the venture amounted to only a comedy of errors. "During its two months' run the show has aroused more lively interest, cynical amusement and sheer pity than possibly any other in history," declared Theodore N. Pockman of the *New York Tribune*, who had traveled with the group.[23] What the media failed to see, argued peace advocates, was that the work of the Neutral Conference for Continuous Mediation continued for another year after the peace ship delegates returned home. In his history of the American peace movement, historian Merle Curti points out that the conference fulfilled a useful purpose, coordinating the "scattered efforts of publicists and idealists in neutral countries engaged in an effort to formulate and popularize terms for a just and lasting peace."[24]

For May, the "spectacular pilgrimage" had been a success, as it had "concentrated the thought of the distracted world upon this hope with a force that assures its achievement." She felt proud of the work done by her and her fellow delegates during their sojourn to seek a permanent peace. "To have advanced its arrival by one hour," May said, "is adequate compensation for the cost in money, time and sacrifices of the Expedition if multiplied a thousandfold."[25] May's sentiments were echoed in part by one of the reporters aboard the *Oscar II*, Elmer Davis. Although he considered the trip a "crazy enterprise," Davis, looking back on the voyage in an essay published in 1939, said that any endeavor, "however visionary and inadequate, to stop a war that was wrecking Europe, appears in retrospect a little less crazy than most of the other purposes that were prevalent in Europe in 1916."[26]

Upon her return to America, May gave numerous lectures attempting to give audiences the true story of the expedition, speaking to church groups, women's clubs, chautauquas, schools, and teacher conventions.[27] As the country inched closer to involvement in World War I, prompted in part by Germany's resumption of unrestricted submarine warfare and the interception of a telegram from German foreign minister Arthur

Zimmermann proposing a German-Mexican alliance against the United States, May continued to plead for peace. In a letter to her friends in Indiana from New York, published after Wilson had asked Congress for a declaration of war on 2 April 1917, May lamented the growing war frenzy on the East Coast and urged her friends back in the Midwest to guard against such an affliction. In addition to New York newspapers clamoring for war, May indicated that meetings were being held daily "whose evident purpose is to bring the public mind to the point of declaring an Anglo-American alliance against the Teuton." Civil and military officials were forcing loyalty oaths upon citizens and women were even organizing into military companies to defend the city against attack. "Where is the psychologist who will not only diagnose the malady that has prostrated the reason, the common sense and the judgment of this community," she asked, "but worse still has paralyzed humane sentiment and Christian principle and obscured that American 'sense of humor' upon which we as a people always rely to preserve our poise under whatever emergency?" She ended her letter: "Hoping that these conditions do not exist in the middle West, I am first, a human; second, a very loyal American; third and always, a loving Hoosier."[28]

May's plea for reason to her former friends and neighbors failed to sway opinion in Indianapolis. With the declaration of war, all things German fell into disrepute. A patriotic fervor gripped Indianapolis and the rest of the state. Teachers were required to take oaths of allegiance in some communities; those who refused were in real danger of losing their jobs for their purported disloyalty. School boards banned the teaching of the German language in public and private schools and German landmarks throughout the state quickly underwent name changes. For example, the Das Deutsche Haus in Indianapolis became the Athenaeum and Bismark Street became Pershing Street. Those who refused to by bonds in Liberty Loan campaigns were even pulled from their homes at night by angry mobs and had their homes painted yellow.[29]

Those who did not share in the enthusiasm at making the world safe for democracy had to endure their friends' contempt even after the war ended in 1918 with an Allied victory. In May's case, her peace activities seemed to make her former neighbors in Indianapolis forget all the good work she had done for the community. Before the war, Adelaide Johnson, a sculptor, feminist, and May's friend, had prepared a bust of the Indianapolis suffragist. In 1919 Ida Husted Harper wrote Grace Julian Clarke that Johnson was in Rome, where she had a studio, finishing work she had started before the war. Harper asked Clarke if she believed that "this would be an opportune time for her to complete the bust of Mrs. Sewall," who had written Harper about the "cordial reception" she had received on her last visit to Indianapolis. "Do you not think that you could now secure enough subscriptions to have the bust completed so that she [Sewall] might see it during her lifetime?" Harper wrote Clarke. "To know that it was placed permanently in Indianapolis would be the greatest compensation that could come to her."[30]

Harper's subsequent correspondence to Clarke about the bust revealed some opposition to honoring May. "I can understand," said Harper, "that there may not be a general desire at present for the bust but in the years to come, after those who have a personal grudge against Mrs. Sewall have passed away, the value of her services to Indianapolis will be better appreciated and people will be glad that they have this reminder of one who is undoubtedly among Indiana's most prominent women, if not the most prominent."[31] Although Harper did not reveal the nature of the personal grudges, a subsequent letter hinted that May's past work on behalf of peace might have been a chief reason for the animus held by some toward her. In January 1920 Harper defended May's patriotism to Clarke, saying she was as loyal to the country as any woman in Indianapolis. Harper did note that May, like Jane Addams, was "almost a fanatic on the subject of peace." Johnson's bust of May remained in storage in Italy; no statue of her was ever erected in Indianapolis.[32]

May's work on behalf of peace, however, gave way within the next few years to another endeavor, one that would cause as much controversy as the Ford Peace Ship. Unknown to the general public May had, since 1897, been deeply involved in spiritualism, communicating with her dead husband Theodore and other deceased relatives. "I knew . . . that I had, so to speak, acquired actual knowledge, if not of immortality," May claimed, "at least of a survival of death—I had learned that the last enemy is destroyed, in that he can destroy neither being nor identity, nor continuity of relationship."[33] In relating her shocking discovery to the public, May had the assistance of an old Indianapolis friend: author Booth Tarkington.

International Council of Women officers gather at the organization's June 1904 meeting in Berlin. May Wright Sewall, wearing an impressive hat, is seated in the first row, fourth from the left. Susan B. Anthony is seated immediately to Sewall's right.

Grace Julian Clarke, May Wright Sewall's friend and fellow supporter of women's rights, served as an officer of the Woman's Franchise League and was president of the Indiana Federation of Clubs.

Indiana State Library

The Scandinavian-American liner Oscar II sets sail on 4 December 1915 from Hoboken, New Jersey. The ship, bound for Christiania, Norway, carried on board delegates from the Ford Peace Mission.

May Wright Sewall (first from right, second row) poses with fellow delegates from the Ford Peace Mission during a recpetion in Christiania, Norway.

Bass Photo Company Collection, Indiana Historical Society, 47282

Robert Dale Owen, son of the founder of New Harmony, Robert Owen, and a respected reformer, diplomat, and politician, pushed for women's rights in the Hoosier State while serving in the Indiana General Assembly. He, like May Wright Sewall, also became involved with spiritualism later in life, publishing such best-selling works as Footfalls on the Boundary of Another World *and* The Debatable Land between This World and the Next.

Hoosier author Booth Tarkington, two-time winner of the Pulitzer Prize, proved to be a powerfull ally for May Wright Sewall and her spiritualist manuscript. Tarkington not only found a publisher for the work, but also provided a thoughtful and sympathetic introduction.

Bobbs-Merrill Company editor Hewitt Howland (standing, right) poses proudly with two of the firm's leading writers, Meredith Nicholson (standing, left) and James Whitcomb Riley.

Portrait of May Wright Sewall used by Bobbs-Merrill Company for promotion of her book
Neither Dead nor Sleeping.

Chapter 6

THE BOOK

In the summer of 1918 Booth Tarkington, enjoying the season at his home in Kennebunkport, Maine, received in the mail an invitation from an old friend from Indianapolis, who was also in Maine, to meet and discuss a manuscript the friend had written. In the letter the friend, May Wright Sewall, did not indicate the subject of her writing, but knowing of her previous work in Indiana, Tarkington assumed that the book would be "something educational." When he finally received the manuscript, the Hoosier writer was astonished to discover "that for more than twenty years this academic-liberal of a thousand human activities . . . had been really living not with the living, so to put it."[1] Writing her with his initial assessment of the work, Tarkington told May he read the manuscript "very carefully and with an ever increasing interest." Calling the book "unique," he added that it proved "its over absolute sincerity from the first, and beyond question; total strangers to you, personally, would recognize that."[2] May's composition, eventually published by the Bobbs-Merrill Company of Indianapolis just two months before her death in July 1920, detailed her extensive experiences in the shadowy world of spiritualism—the belief in the possibility of the living communicating with the dead.

May's communion with the deceased, which included not only extensive conversations with her husband Theodore but also interactions with a medieval priest and a famous musician, shocked many who knew the no-nonsense suffragette and reformer. Anton Scherrer, a columnist for the *Indianapolis Times*, said that nothing "rocked the foundations of Indianapolis quite as much" as the appearance of May's publication, because nobody in her old hometown knew about her contacts with the spirit world.[3] In fact, only a dozen or so people knew about this facet of May's life. During her communications with her departed husband, he had warned her, May told a reporter from the *Indianapolis Star*, not to relate them "to the world until she had them in such form the world could understand them." Also, those to whom she related her experiences often expressed the belief that May suffered from a mental delusion. Perhaps realizing that she would be ridiculed by many for her otherworldly experiences, which first occurred in 1897, May decided to relate her spiritualist story to the world only when "extreme feebleness" had taken her once and for all out of public affairs. Free from the various commitments to reform activities she had engaged in for most of her life, May had time to cull from the hundreds of her record books the spiritualist experiences she related in *Neither Dead nor Sleeping*.[4]

The question of whether it was possible to communicate with the dead had been hotly debated in American society since 1848 when the Fox sisters—Katherine, age eleven, and Margaretta, age thirteen—had reported strange rappings and knockings in their family's home in Hydesville, New York. The children's parents, John and Margaret Fox, soon spread word of the strange occurrences to neighbors, who came to the home and themselves heard the odd noises. Years later both sisters confessed that they, and not disembodied spirits, were the cause of the rappings. The Fox sisters' confessions came too late, however, to stop a nationwide spiritualist movement that unlike organized religion, which promoted contact with the deity only through a select priesthood, promised instead to render "heaven utterly democratic and accessible to all." In 1868 the American Association of Spiritualists had organized, and by 1871 spiritualist societies had been formed in twenty-two states.[5]

The Hoosier State was not immune to the siren call from the grave. In 1862 the first organization of Indiana spiritualists was created with Dr. Samuel Maxwell of Richmond as president. Two years earlier, Robert Dale Owen, son of the founder of New Harmony, Robert Owen, and a respected reformer, diplomat, and politician, published *Footfalls on the Boundary of Another World*. The book, which quickly sold out of its first printing of two thousand copies, contained narratives of such phenomena as hauntings, clairvoyance, and somnambulism. In 1872 Owen followed up his previous success by writing another best-selling spiritualist book, *The Debatable Land between This World and the Next*, which attempted to Christianize spiritualism. He argued that it was essential that the entire subject of spiritualism "should be studied in its broad phase as one of the vital elements of an enlightened Christian faith." By 1888 the Indiana Association of Spiritualists decided to build a campground for its meetings and selected Chesterfield as the site. The thirty-four-acre site hosted its first meeting in 1892 and grew to become the second largest spiritualist camp in the country (only Lily Dale in New York was larger) and averaged crowds of twenty thousand people at its annual six-week sessions during the summer.[6]

In spite of the enthusiastic reception spiritualism received in some quarters, to most the movement remained a subject for ridicule, largely associated as it was with "socialism, atheism, and free love."[7] But for suffragists spiritualists were kindred spirits who shared their belief in equal rights for all and who invited them to speak at their gatherings. Spiritualists were the only religious group in the world, claimed suffrage leaders, that "recognized the equality of women."[8] It was at a spiritualist camp meeting in Lily Dale, New York, that May began to commune with the spirits. The seeds for her communications with the deceased had been planted years before during some of the darkest days of her life. A fortnight before her husband Theodore Sewall's death on 23 December 1895, he had told her that his death was inevitable. "I wish now only to say that if I discover that I survive death," said Theodore Sewall, "the first thing I shall do will be to ascertain whether or not Jesus ever returned to earth after His crucifixion. You know we have not believed it; but, if I find that He did return to His disciples, I shall do nothing else until I shall have succeeded in returning to you, unless before that time, you have come to me."[9]

After her husband's death, May tried to forget her grief by burying herself in her work, including her administrative and teaching roles at the Girls' Classical School. She succeeded so well that she put Theodore Sewall's deathbed declaration completely out of her mind. When some Indianapolis friends advised her to visit a local medium in able to see and talk again with her husband, the proposal shocked her. "It seemed to me grossly to violate both reason and delicacy," she said. Instead of taking them up on their offer, May continued to give her time to her school and work with both the National and International Council of Women. While at a speaking engagement in Nova Scotia in June 1897, she received an invitation to give a talk at a "Woman's Day" program at what she later learned was a spiritualist camp in Lily Dale, New York. "I had held myself so aloof from all means of information about spiritualism," May said, "that I did not know there were such camps."[10]

May arrived at Lily Dale's assembly grounds at 7:00 P.M. on 9 August 1897 and was greeted by the chairman of the press committee for the National American Woman Suffrage Association, who asked her if she wished to tour the facility and be introduced to some of the famous mediums gathered there for the meeting. "I told her," said May, "that I did not wish to meet any 'medium' however 'famous'; that to me the word was offensive, being synonymous in my opinion, with the words, deceiver, pretender, charlatan and ignoramus. I frankly asserted that the name and the office assumed by those bearing it were equally obnoxious to delicacy and to intelligence." Although her audience the next day proved to be "attentive, responsive and sympathetic," May wanted nothing more than to depart the place for her next speaking engagement at Chautauqua, New York.[11]

A series of unexpected difficulties, however, caused May to stay over at Lily Dale for a time. Giving in to a "compelling impulse which I scarcely realized until I acted upon it," she participated in a sitting with a famous independent slate writer, a medium who used slates to convey messages from the spirits to their intended recipients. During her meeting with the slate writer, May claimed that the blank slates never left her possession, but when she returned with them to her hotel she discovered that they were covered with "clear and legible writing" and contained "perfectly coherent, intelligent and characteristic replies to questions which I had written upon bits of paper that had not passed out of my hands." Through this experience, May said she had acquired "actual knowledge, if not of immortality, at least of a survival of death—I had learned that the last enemy is destroyed, in that he can destroy neither being nor identity, nor continuity of relationship." Through subsequent sittings with slate writers, trance readers, a trumpet medium, a psychometrist, and other "richly endowed and variously developed psychics," May communicated with a number of her deceased loved ones, including her husband Theodore, father, mother, half-sister, great-grandfather, niece, and two sisters-in-law.[12]

Through the years, as she became more attuned to the spirit world, May communicated with her deceased former husband herself through automatic writing. Equipped with only a tablet and pencil, May would sit in her library and her husband's spirit would guide her hand to produce written answers to her questions about life beyond the grave. These amazing messages, she later told the *Indianapolis Star*, came to her as impressions upon her mind. May noted that the experience was as though she received "a blow on the brain—not physically of course—but clear and distinct and without warning. And in an instant comes a complete train of thought—swift—immediate—not arrived at by the slow and ordinary sequence of ideas—a complete train of thought solving some heretofore unsolvable riddle of the universe." These thoughts could not have come from her own mind, she insisted, for they often concerned themes that she had never imagined in her whole life. "I have the sure belief," said May, "that they are sent to me by other minds which, because of the knowledge they have gained beyond the veil, are enabled to think in complete circles and to present a thought to me complete."[13]

During her conversations with her husband's spirit, May constantly received the message to "study science." As she gained more and more experience with the spirit world, May began to draw certain conclusions about this miraculous form of communication. According to May, these included the following:

First: While every one after passing out of the flesh realizes the continuance of life, the vividness of the realization varies with different people.

Second: Although all perceive that life is continuous, not all realize that it is sequential.

Third: Large numbers of people, realizing the continuance of love, as well as of life, and finding that they possess the power of unfettered movement from place to place, often do visit the Earth Plane and persistently endeavor to induce in their friends a consciousness of their presence.

Fourth: The majority of those who have passed on are, without aid, as unable to reach the friends who remain on earth as these are, unaided, to reach those who have experienced death; and they suffer from inaccessibility of surviving friends as these suffer from bereavement. It seems probable, however, that their grief is mitigated by their knowledge.

Fifth: The deceased can obtain assistance through unusually developed excarnates, as we on this plane can get help from similarly unusually developed humans still incarnate. The two such unusually developed beings serving their respective patrons may be compared to the "transmitter" and "receiver" employed in wireless telegraphy, each being in turn both transmitter and receiver.[14]

Through a series of lectures, Theodore Sewall imparted to May information about the great mystery of how spirits return and communicate with the living. From the beginning of historic time, he told his wife, there have been "devout and God-fearing" people who possessed the knowledge of the immortality of the soul. Such knowledge had been gained, he said, exactly as information about a foreign country had been gained—"by going thither or by receiving thence intelligent guests capable of giving an accurate account of what they have witnessed and experienced." Once a spirit is freed by death from its fleshy bonds, it discovers "every mental emotional and spiritual aptitude quickened" and, if the spirit had strong ties with those still living, "it sets about the task of readjusting its relationships," including direct contact.[15]

In addition to teaching her about the spirit world, Theodore Sewall introduced May to distinct spirits, including Anton Rubinstein, a famed pianist, and Père Condé, a medieval priest and physician from France. Although May never considered herself musical, Theodore Sewall insisted that she buy a piano on which to be instructed by Rubinstein. Her husband told her that the deepest element in her character was a love of harmony. "It is your love of harmony which makes you always reconcile the different," he told May. "It is this which enabled you to conceive of 'the Council Idea,' and which has given you your success as an organizer. You have always been an organizer and now your reward is to be instructed by the Master of Harmony." For his part, Condé placed May on a strict regimen of massage, baths, and exercise. Already a vegetarian, May also followed a strict diet imposed on her by Condé. She claimed that these measures not only improved her eyesight so much that she could read without spectacles, but also restored her to perfect health after having being diagnosed by a doctor in 1901 as having an incurable illness (Bright's disease). In time, May felt her acquaintance with these spirits seemed "more intimate and reciprocally comprehending than do my relations with any equal number of friends still incarnate selected from my entire list of acquaintances; their personalities also are more sharply differentiated to my perceptions." One spirit, who identified himself as Franz Mesmer, the great magician, even displayed himself to her early one morning in 1903 when May was teaching an English class at the Girls' Classical School.[16]

May's remarkable account of her communications with the spirit world became known to the living through the unstinting efforts of an Indiana writer who had had his own experience with unexplained phenomena: Tarkington. When he was fourteen years old and living in Indianapolis, Tarkington discovered that his sister, Hauté, had psychic powers. The Tarkington family hosted séances at its home that drew such distinguished visitors as James Whitcomb Riley. Although Hauté's powers faded away after her marriage, her devoted brother remained convinced of the reality of his experiences. Throughout his life, noted Tarkington biographer James Woodress, the writer "was tolerant of other persons' alleged supersensory experience."[17] When May approached him for assistance in finding a publisher for her spiritualist manuscript, Tarkington proved eager to help.

By the fall of 1918 Tarkington had a stenographer make a copy of May's manuscript to present to possible publishers. He wrote May that he needed to find a firm willing not only to print the book, but also to promote it effectively as well. "I assure you that I will do everything within my power not only to get it printed," he said, "but to get it 'pushed'!" Tarkington reiterated his belief that May's manuscript stood as a "unique document with the air of a classic in human experience."[18] By March 1919 Tarkington had decided to place the manuscript with the Bobbs-Merrill Company, which could trace its roots in Indianapolis back to the 1850s and was the publisher for such Hoosier literary lions as Riley, George Ade, Meredith Nicholson, and Maurice Thompson. Tarkington passed along May's manuscript to Bobbs-Merrill with the understanding that he would write an introduction for the book. He did warn May that a decision on whether or not to publish her work would take some time.[19]

Tarkington's warning proved to be prophetic. During the spring and summer, he exchanged a series of letters with May discussing the lack of a decision from Bobbs-Merrill on the book. Although the firm's literary adviser and trade editor Hewitt H. Howland had told Tarkington he was in favor of accepting the book, and Tarkington wrote May that he was tempted to push the firm about the manuscript, he feared doing so because a "very little push upon a publisher sometimes turns him aside from the right path." A final decision on the manuscript depended upon the opinion of William C. Bobbs, the company's president, "and that must take its own time not ours!" said Tarkington.[20] By the end of July, Tarkington's patience had been tried enough for him to suggest to May that she write a note to Howland "and hint that you can wait no longer." If Bobbs-Merrill did decide against publishing her work, Tarkington told May that he had already opened discussions with a literary adviser for another publisher, and he had expressed "much interest" in her manuscript.[21]

Sometime in August Bobbs-Merrill finally agreed to publish May's spiritualist book. One of the reasons for the firm's acceptance might have been its eagerness to add Tarkington to its list of authors. According to one account, David Laurance Chambers, a Bobbs-Merrill editor and later the company's president, was Tarkington's intimate friend and "never concealed his hope that the author might some day publish through Bobbs-

Merrill."[22] For his part, Tarkington continued to advise the suffragist, sending her suggestions on how to conduct contract negotiations with the Indianapolis publishing firm. "I am sure he [Howland] will be fair and the terms will be customary—it is always about the same thing: 10% gross, I suppose, on sales up to 10,000 and 15% thereafter—some such arrangement," he wrote May. "I should let him propose the terms and, if they are like this, accept at once." The Hoosier writer went on to tell May not to believe that his "small" contribution had induced Bobbs-Merrill to accept the book. His efforts on her behalf did perhaps increase the firm's interest in reviewing the manuscript, but it was the work "itself, and nothing else whatever, that has brought them to their favorable decision."[23]

During her exchange of letters with Tarkington about her manuscript, the seventy-five-year-old May, who had been in ill health, had been making plans to leave the East Coast and return to live in Indianapolis. She had even written her old suffragist friend, Grace Julian Clarke, to seek advice on possible places for her to stay. Clarke wrote back expressing her delight at May's decision to live again in Indianapolis, but reported that the three places she had in mind as possible locations for May to take up residence were unavailable. Although she expressed her willingness to continue searching for lodgings, Clarke made it clear that there was no room for May in her own home. "I have competent help for my own immediate family, but cannot think of enlarging it," Clarke wrote May. "I shall hope that you may be near enough for me to see you often, however, and am very happy that you are so far restored as to be able to come back home."[24]

Undeterred by Clarke's bad news about lodgings for her, May remained resolved to return to Indianapolis, the scene of many of the triumphs and tragedies in her life. Writing from the Aloha Rest home in Winthrop Highlands, Massachusetts, May expressed to Howland, the editor for her book, her gratitude for accepting her manuscript, adding that it pleased her to have the book published in the city where many of the experiences took place and where there were many witnesses to the "external regimen and to the changes in myself" recorded in the volume. While giving her consent to Howland to shorten the second part of the book, she did ask him one favor. May indicated she was quite anxious to have the book come out as soon as possible because numerous publishing firms, including the most conservative ones, were issuing books on spiritualism in order to take advantage of the huge surge in interest in the subject from families who had lost loved ones during World War I. "The war has terribly increased the number of bereaved and bleeding hearts and often the skepticism of the intellect can be broken down only through the agony of a yearning heart," she said. "I, who have suffered, want to help those who do suffer."[25]

In early October 1919 May finally returned to Indianapolis, taking up residence at a convalescent home at 1732 N. Illinois St. Although so ill with heart disease that she had trouble breathing and had to be propped up in bed by pillows, May, looked after by some of her former students at the Girls' Classical School, managed to make corrections on galley proofs of her book.[26] In spite of her illness, there were times when the old confident May again flashed into being. "I think I never did a better piece of proof reading—and I am perfectly delighted with the book," she told Howland in December. "I know it will have an ultimate great success."[27] May's renewed confidence may have been inspired by the rapport she established with her editor. She apologized to Howland for hindering the work on her book because of her illness, but promised to keep herself well enough to correct proof as fast as it arrived. May was lucky in her new association, for she would be working with an editor known for selecting and publishing manuscripts that had the most potential as best sellers for the firm.[28]

An Indianapolis native, Howland had an impressive pedigree; his father served as a judge and his brother, Louis, worked as an editor for the *Indianapolis News*. His father's death dashed Hewitt Howland's hopes for a college education, so at age fifteen he took a job in the Yohn Book Shop on Washington Street. After traveling in Great Britain for a time, Howland returned to Indianapolis and worked as a railway clerk and broker. In 1898 he started working for Bobbs-Merrill as a part time manuscript reader, becoming an editor just two years later. "His rise in the firm," noted a history of Bobbs-Merrill, "was meteoric." In spite of his talent, Howland, who went on to become editor of *Century Magazine,* preferred to remain in the background, seldom achieving the visibility enjoyed by Bobbs and

Chambers. Still, Howland's work caught the attention of the press. In 1910 the *Indianapolis Star* reported that in its editor Bobbs-Merrill had an employee who was known across the country for producing best sellers with "the dash, brilliancy and acumen that are consonant with all successes of the twentieth century." The newspaper went on to say that Howland pos-sessed "a genius for literary values that seems almost intuition, combined with a culture that is fundamental. To these are added charm of manner and the gentle art of letter writing, the whole superimposed on a vast capacity for hard work."[29]

For his part, Howland used his charm and skill as an editor to forge a solid relationship with his new author: May. He offered few major changes to her manuscript, even deciding against some deletions in part two that he had suggested earlier. Howland did, however, object to some aspects of May's preface, including a part where she expressed the hope that men and women trained in scientific investigation would take up where she left off. "This will lead the dear average reader to feel that the book is not intended for him and I am sure you want him to read it," Howland told May. "You don't want to discourage him by conveying the impression that it [the book] is intended primarily for trained scientific investigators."[30] May thanked Howland for his suggestions, and even rewrote the preface to alleviate his concerns. "If you feel it can be further improved I shall be glad to act on any suggestion you may make," she said.[31]

Forced out of public affairs by poor health and her dedication to seeing her book published, May nevertheless caught the attention of the local media. Learning of her return to her hometown, the *Indianapolis News* took the opportunity to question her about a variety of subjects, including world affairs and woman's suffrage. Turning to one of her favorite subjects, the quest for peace, May told the *News* that such a goal would be brought about by "spiritual reformation, by the movement of the soul, not by the use of ammunition." Although she expressed support for a League of Nations, she said the organization as it then stood was "very defective." Although the Nineteenth Amedment, giving women the right to vote, still needed to be ratified by the states, May said she had considered the issue settled since 1889 and was now anxious to see what women would do once they formally had the ballot. "I have no reason to believe," she said, "that they will use it differently from the way in which men make use of it. Why should they? We are all very much alike, born of the same parents."[32]

As winter turned into spring and her book remained unpublished, May began to be apprehensive about the future. "I beg you to believe," she said in a dictated letter to Howland, "that I am distressed at feeling the need of troubling you, but I have been very ill for several weeks with the prospect of continuing so, or worse; and I am beginning to be very anxious about the possibility of holding out until my book is out." She went on to say that she did not know if he could do anything to hurry the process, but was sure that if "you could know my distressing situation you would be sympathetically anxious to try and hurry it."[33] May's friends were also worried about her health. Ida Husted Harper confided to Clarke that she had been "feeling very uneasy about her [Sewall], as she has not written me for weeks and did not even acknowledge my Christmas message, which is most unusual for her."[34] By the time Howland could present May with a complimentary copy of her book on 8 May, she had been moved from her Illinois Street residence to Room 131 at Saint Vincent's Hospital. With the help of a nurse, May dictated a letter to Howland thanking him for the copy of her book and offering her appreciation for all of his help and kindness through the publishing process. "Owing to my condition," May added, "it has sometimes seemed hard for me to wait and I fear I may have manifested a very unworthy impatience. I trust to your charity to forget it if I have done so." She regretted that her ill health prevented her from proceeding with a second book, this one about "theoric painting."[35]

In answering May's letter, Howland attempted to deflect her praise for his efforts on behalf of her book, telling her what he did had been done "with pleasure and affection. If the book in its appearance pleases you I am happy and well repaid; the future is to some extent on the knees of the gods, but we shall keep the ancient divinities stirred up, so that they may not nod or neglect their opportunities." He predicted that May's book was "destined to make a profound impression, and to do more to convince the unbelieving than any human document yet given to the world."[36] To help Howland's prediction come true, Bobbs-Merrill placed its considerable promotional muscle squarely behind *Neither Dead nor Sleeping.* Calling the work "The Wonder Book of the Ages," and labeling its author "one of the best known among the pioneer progressive women of the country," the firm issued a first printing of three thousand copies and promoted it to book dealers as "a sure-fire seller from the start. It's the kind the dealer will take home and read and reread himself!" The Indianapolis company had May autograph copies of the book, which sold for $3, to be sent to influential literary editors representing such publications as the *Literary Digest, Publishers Weekly,* and *Booklist,* as well as newspapers in New York, Chicago, Los Angeles, and San Francisco. She also prepared signed copies for such influential figures as William Randolph Hearst and his wife. These promotional efforts paid off; Howland reported to May that ten to twelve newspapers had printed a full-page story on the book and as of early June one-third of the first printing of three thousand had been sold. He predicted a bright outlook for the book and indicated that the firm's confidence and interest remained unabated.[37]

Although still in ill health, May displayed considerable interest in her book's promotion, even subscribing to a clipping service to check on reviews.[38] She also found the strength to discuss her spiritualist experiences with a reporter, Elizabeth Morgan, with the *Indianapolis Star.* The resulting full-page article in the *Star's* Sunday magazine had featured some optimistic predictions from May about spiritualism's future, including its eventual teaching as a subject in high schools and universities. "To me psychic science has already become so simple that I feel confident of being able to put its laws into the sort of words and sentences even very young people can understand," May told Morgan. "Only my enforced feebleness keeps me from starting something of the kind, as a test, in some progressive school." Morgan, who interviewed May a few weeks before *Neither Dead nor Sleeping's* publication, said the former teacher radiated an eagerness that those who read the book might profit from her experiences and gain from it "the sure comfort of knowing the simplicity and naturalness of the life into which they passed from the life of earth."[39]

As someone who had worked throughout her life for the betterment of the human condition, May realized that to many the emphasis she placed on her psychic experiences might pale in comparison to such world problems as hunger and disease. In an interview with May that Bobbs-Merrill provided as part of its promotional efforts for her book, the reformer admitted that the world offered "huge problems for the solving and the human mind can be applied—should be applied—to all of them." Still, she asked if there was any reason why those interested in "helping this world as they pass through it should not seek to know of that world to which they are surely and rapidly traveling? Does God expect us to be blind and deaf to those great truths which exist whether we allow ourselves to admit them or not?" To her, those things that had to do with the "eternity to come" were much more vital than the passing things of everyday experience. "None of us want to pass into oblivion," May said. "Then why close our eyes and ears to such revelations as are coming to us every day. It is almost as though this was the era when the veil should gradually begin to lift and all who cared to see might glimpse the things that are."[40]

To ease the reader into the story of her astonishing experiences, Tarkington had contributed a compelling and open-minded introduction for *Neither Dead nor Sleeping*. In reading May's story, Tarkington said it seemed to him that her struggle to cure her illness and make herself a proper messenger for the dead were recorded not as a person living in the modern world, but as "some medieval penitent, feeding upon snow by day and lying prayerful upon a bed of cinders at night, seeking to become a spirit." Considering the validity of May's spiritualist beliefs, Tarkington had three possible explanations for her story:

1. Mrs. Sewall is laboring under a hallucination, or a series of hallucinations, continuing more than twenty years.
2. The communications purporting to be from the dead are really the work of an inner self of hers, sometimes called a subconscious. This is, or is related to, the part of our minds that constructs our dreams; and is capable of far more wonderful performances than most psychologists yet admit to be demonstrated.
3. The communications are, as Mrs. Sewall believes them to be, from people we speak of as dead; but really they live.

For Tarkington, the truth of the matter rested somewhere between the second and third explanations. Although there may have been some professional mediums who "imposed" on her, they constituted "only a trifle in the narrative." When it came to May herself as a medium for communicating with the dead, Tarkington said that either her subconscious had been "up to a dumbfounding prodigy of dream-building, or else Mrs. Sewall has been in communication with living people whom we have thought of as dead."[41]

Many reviewers echoed Tarkington's sympathetic treatment of May's work. Writing for the *Chicago Tribune*, Elia W. Peattie claimed that the book had been written in "good faith" by a "gentlewoman of high veracity." The author had found, Peattie added, an "escape from illness and sorrow, and there remains but to extend to her sincere and deeply felt congratulations."[42] Reviewing several books on psychic experiences for the *New York Evening Post*, J. Keith Torbert wrote that both for those who believe and for those who scoff at spiritualism May's book "has essentials to reveal." *Neither Dead nor Sleeping* had, Torbert added, something that raised it above the ordinary. "This is the very human touch to the writing," he wrote. "The strong, admirable character of Mrs. Sewall appears on every page." There may be some who believe the author had been on the "road to insanity," but the reviewer noted that there seemed "to have been a remarkable amount of common sense displayed as she traveled."[43] May's work even received a positive notice in the *New York Times Book Review*. In reviewing eleven books that discussed the question of what happens after a person dies, the *Review* highlighted May's as "one of the most striking—amazing is hardly too strong a word."[44]

These vindications of her work came as May, now seventy-six years old, lay gravely ill in her room at Saint Vincent's Hospital, where she finally died at 11:15 P.M. on 22 July 1920. The *Indianapolis Star* reported that May's age, taken in connection "with a gradual physical decline manfesting [sic] itself in the last three months convinced her physicians some time ago that her recovery was impossible." After funeral services at All Souls Unitarian Church, overseen by Rev. S. C. Wicks, May was buried alongside her beloved husband, Theodore Sewall, at Crown Hill Cemetery.[45] In the death of May Wright Sewall, the *Indianapolis News* said on its editorial page, the world lost a citizen. Although she had lived, worked, and died in Indianapolis, her "activities were such that she was known not only in this country but throughout Europe as well." Throughout her life, "Mrs. Sewall possessed the faculty of transmitting her boundless enthusiasm and her original ideas to the world around her. One could not slumber in her presence for her vitality was contagious."[46]

Ill as she was during the last few days of her life, May still managed to reach out to her friends. Harper noted that May had asked one of her relatives to make sure she received "a beautiful silver backcomb, which I have seen her wear many times, and in asking him to do this she [Sewall] added the words: 'I think it would be very becoming to Mrs. Harper,' which much increased its value." In addition to bequeathing to friends her worldly goods—Clarke received a tea table at which numerous guests had been entertained at the Sewalls' famous gatherings in their Indianapolis home—May also attempted to ensure that her life received the attention she believed it deserved. Not long before May's death, Harper, author of a three-volume biography of Susan B. Anthony, received an undated letter from the Indianapolis suffragist "in which she referred to a box of material which she was leaving me to be used in her 'biography' and referring to me as her 'biographer.'" Unfortunately for May, Harper had had enough of biography for a time, writing Clarke that nothing could induce her to undertake such a task.[47]

In the years following May's death, however, there were attempts made in Indianapolis to commemorate her achievements. At the February 1921 meeting in Indianapolis of the State Collegiate Alumnae, James Woodburn, an Indiana University history professor and close friend of both Sewalls for many years, presented a talk outlining May's career. In addition, plans were discussed by May's friends and admirers to honor her memory by naming a bookshelf in her honor at the local library and dedicating a pair of elaborate bronze lamps and standards in her name at the entrance to the John Herron Art Institute.[48] On a rainy Sunday afternoon in May 1923, two bronze memorial candelabra were dedicated in May's memory at Herron Art Institute. At the dedication ceremony, held indoors at the institute due to the inclement weather, Woodburn praised May for giving "her soul in self-surrender to the service of humanity. She appealed to a world spirit as against a national or race spirit. Her ideal aim was to escape from provincialism and to realize the unity of humanity." Other speakers detailed May's achievements with the Girls' Classical School, the Indianapolis Woman's Club, the Contemporary Club, and the International Council of Women.[49]

Looking back on her life, May had much to be thankful for, she related to Clarke the Thanksgiving before her death. Her heart, Clarke remembered May saying, was "full of gratitude" for being a native of the United States rather than any other country; being born in a family of "liberal tendencies, liberals in politics and religion"; being endowed with a good mind and body that enabled her to "keep going at least beyond the Scriptural span of years"; having a husband (Theodore Sewall) "whose tastes and ideals were in entire sympathy with her own"; and possessing the capacity for loving her friends. "I was struck with the emphasis she placed on this," Clarke said of May, "and the fact that it was the capacity for loving, rather than the capacity for making others love her, that she stressed." May believed that the capacity for loving "was more worth while because it was a means of growth; and growth, development, was the ultimate end of life," Clarke observed. Finally, May told Clarke she was thankful for being "an active factor in the world, not a drone or an idle spectator. She had been an integer, not a fraction, a positive, not a negative quantity." Although during her last days May recognized, Clarke related, that she "was a member of the Has Been family, but it comforted her that she was a HAS BEEN, a plus, not a minus. Another . . . instance of the value she placed on *activity*." All of May's activity, however, shared one goal: to make herself useful to the world at large, a task she accomplished. "What she wrought," Clarke said of May, "will endure, and generations yet unborn will find life a fuller and richer experience because she joined in the effort to make it so instead of supinely accepting conditions as they were."[50]

Notes

Preface
[1] Nelson Price, "The Century's 10 Greatest Hoosiers," *Indianapolis Star,* 19 December 1999.
[2] Elbert Hubbard to May Wright Sewall, 24 November 1897, May Wright Sewall Papers, Indianapolis–Marion County Public Library, Indianapolis.

Prologue
[1] May Wright Sewall, "Indiana," in Elizabeth Cady Stanton, Susan B. Anthony, and Matilda Joslyn Gage, eds., *History of Woman Suffrage* 6 vols. (1886; reprint, Salem, N.H.: Ayer Company, 1985), 3:551.
[2] Susan Vogelgesang, "Zerelda Wallace: Indiana's Conservative Radical," *Traces of Indiana and Midwestern History* 4 (summer 1992):37–38.
[3] Clifton J. Phillips, "May Eliza Wright Sewall," in Edward T. James, Janet Wilson James, and Paul S. Boyer, eds. *Notable American Women, 1607–1950: A Biographical Dictionary* 3 vols. (Cambridge, Mass.: The Belknap Press of Harvard University Press, 1971), 3:269–70.
[4] Bertha Damaris Knobe, "Mrs. May Wright Sewall: 'Leader of 5,000,000 Women,'" *Harper's Bazaar*, 2 June 1900, 278–81.
[5] Ida Husted Harper, "Mrs. Sewall's Place in Woman Movement," in George Cottman's Biographical Scrapbook, Indiana Division, Indiana State Library, vol. 6, 83–84.
[6] See, Inez Haynes Irwin, *Angels and Amazons: A Hundred Years of American Women* (Garden City, N.Y.: Doubleday, Doran and Company, 1933), 229, and Hester Anne Hale, "May (Mary Eliza Wright) Sewall," in Robert G. Barrows and David Bodenhamer, eds., *Encyclopedia of Indianapolis* (Bloomington: Indiana University Press, 1994), 1,253–54.
[7] "Mrs. Sewall, 76, Educator, Dead at St. Vincent's," *Indianapolis Star*, 23 July 1920.
[8] Mary McLaughlin Reminiscences, Manuscript Section, Indiana State Library, Indianapolis.
[9] *History of Woman Suffrage*, 3:535–6.
[10] Anton Scherrer, "Lack of Feminine World Similar to Fraternal Led Our

Good Women to do Something About it in 1882," *Indianapolis Times,* 3 December 1938.

[11] Knobe, "Mrs. May Wright Sewall," 281.

[12] Jane Stephens, "May Wright Sewall: An Indiana Reformer," *Indiana Magazine of History* 78 (December 1982):278–9.

[13] Charlotte Cathcart, *Indianapolis from Our Old Corner* (Indianapolis: Indiana Historical Society, 1965), 21–23.

[14] "Started By Enemies. Report Calculated to Injure Girls' Classical School," *Indianapolis Sentinel,* 6 April 1902.

[15] Stephens, "May Wright Sewall," 281.

[16] Knobe, "Mrs. May Wright Sewall," 280.

[17] "Our October Cover Page: Mrs. May Wright Sewall," *The Ladies Review,* October 1916, 172.

[18] Booth Tarkington, "Introduction," in May Wright Sewall, *Neither Dead nor Sleeping* (Indianapolis: Bobbs-Merrill Company, 1920), n.p.

[19] Sewall, *Neither Dead nor Sleeping,* 5.

[20] Knobe, "Mrs. May Wright Sewall," 279–80.

[21] May Wright Sewall, *Women, World War and Permanent Peace* (San Francisco: John J. Newbergin, 1915), xii. See also, Barbara Jane Stephens, "May Wright Sewall (1844–1920)," Ph.D. diss., Ball State University, May 1977, 168.

[22] Stephens, "May Wright Sewall," *IMH,* 291–92.

[23] Henry Ford to May Wright Sewall, 27 November 1915, Telegrams, Letters and Other Documents Relating to the Ford Expedition, 1915–1916, Manuscript Section, ISL.

[24] Burnet Hershey, *The Odyssey of Henry Ford and the Great Peace Ship* (New York: Taplinger Publishing Company, 1967), 86.

[25] May Wright Sewall, "To My Friends in Hoosierdom," 16 December 1915, Ford Expedition, Manuscript Section, ISL.

[26] Irwin, *Angels and Amazons,* 229.

[27] "Mrs. May Wright Sewall: Sketch of Her Work," *Indianapolis Sentinel,* 6 April 1902.

[28] Grace Julian Clarke, "May Wright Sewall: In Memoriam," Grace Julian Clarke Papers, Manuscript Section, ISL.

[29] Ida Husted Harper, *Life and Work of Susan B. Anthony,* 3 vols. (1898; reprint, New York: Arno and the New York Times, 1969), 2:850.

[30] Sewall, *Neither Dead nor Sleeping,* 1.

[31] Ibid., 3–4.

[32] Ibid., 9–10.

[33] Elizabeth Morgan, "Miss May Wright Sewall Tells of Talks with Departed Mate," *Indianapolis Star*, 9 May 1920.

[34] Anton Scherrer, "Book by Mrs. May Wright Sewall Revealing Talks With Dead Husband Caused a Sensation Back in 1920," *Indianapolis Times*, 11 April 1939.

[35] Morgan, "Miss May Wright Sewall Tells of Talks with Departed Mate."

[36] Ann Braude, *Radical Spirits: Spiritualism and Women's Rights in Nineteenth-Century America* (Boston: Beacon Press, 1989), 2–3.

[37] Barbara Goldsmith, *Other Powers: The Age of Suffrage, Spiritualism, and the Scandalous Victoria* Woodhull (New York: Alfred Knopf, 1998), xiii.

[38] Tarkington, "Introduction," in Sewall, *Neither Dead Nor Sleeping*, n.p.

[39] Dr. James Woodburn, "Mrs. Sewall—Servant of Humanity," *Indianapolis Star*, 22 February 1921.

Chapter 1

[1] See, Geoffrey C. Ward and Ken Burns, *Not for Ourselves Alone: The Story of Elizabeth Cady Stanton and Susan B. Anthony* (New York: Alfred A. Knopf, 1999), 39–41; Ellen Carol DuBois, *Feminism and Suffrage: The Emergence of an Independent Women's Movement in America, 1848–1869* (Ithaca, N.Y.: Cornell University Press, 1978), 23–24; and Marjorie Spruill Wheeler, "A Short History of the Woman Suffrage Movement in America," in Wheeler, ed., *One Woman, One Vote: Rediscovering the Woman Suffrage Movement* (Troutdale, Ore.: NewSage Press, 1995), 9–19.

[2] Aileen S. Kraditor, *The Ideas of the Woman Suffrage Movement*, 1890–1920 (1965; reprint, New York: W.W. Norton & Company, 1981), 4.

[3] Emma Lou Thornbrough, *Indiana in the Civil War Era*, 1850–1880 (1965; reprint, Indianapolis: Indiana Historical Society, 1989), 34. The remark from the delegate to the Constitutional Convention was sparked by a proposal from Robert Dale Owen to include in the new state constitution the right for women to acquire property. Ibid.

[4] Barbara Janes Stephens, "May Wright Sewall (1844–1920)," Ph.D diss., Ball State University, May 1977, 7.

[5] Hester Anne Hale, "May Wright Sewall: Avowed Feminist," Indiana Historical Society, Indianapolis, Chapter 1, Page 6.

[6] Merica E. Hoagland, "Mrs. May Wright Sewall—An Appreciation," 6 April 1933, Manuscript Section, Indiana State Library, Indianapolis.

[7] See "Mrs. May Wright Sewall" in Frances A. Willard and Mary A. Livermore, eds. *A Woman of the Century: Fourteen Hundred-Seventy Biographical Sketches*

Accompanied by Portraits of Leading American Women in All Walks of Life (Buffalo: Charles Wells Moulton, 1893), 644.

[8] *Woman's News,* 13 February 1892. See also, *Pictorial and Biographical Memoirs of Indianapolis and Marion County, Indiana* (Chicago: Goodspeed Brothers, 1893), 322–25. See also, Clifton J. Phillips, "May Eliza Wright Sewell," in Edward T. James, ed., *Notable American Women, 1607–1950: A Biographical Dictionary* 3 vols. (Cambridge, Mass.: The Belknap Press of Harvard University Press, 1971), 3:269–71; Hester Anne Hale, "May (Mary Eliza) Wright Sewall," in Robert G. Barrows and David Bodenhamer, eds., *Encyclopedia of Indianapolis* (Bloomington: Indiana University Press, 1994), 1,253–54; and James Woodburn, "Mrs. Sewall—Servant of Humanity," *Indianapolis Star,* 22 February 1921.

[9] Eleanor Flexner and Ellen Fitzpatrick, *Century of Struggle: The Woman's Rights Movement in the United States* (1959; reprint, Cambridge, Mass.: The Belknap Press of Harvard University Press, 1996), 22.

[10] Robert C. Nesbit and William F. Thompson, *Wisconsin: A History,* 2d ed. (Madison, Wis.: The University of Wisconsin Press, 1989), 230.

[11] Jerry Apps, *One-Room Country Schools: History and Recollections from Wisconsin* (Amherst, Wis.: Amherst Press, 1996), 9. See also, Nancy Woloch, *Women and the American Experience* (1984; reprint, New York: McGraw-Hill, 1994), 246.

[12] Hester Anne Hale, "Which May Wright Sewall Are You Talking About?", Indianapolis Woman's Club Papers, IHS.

[13] See, Dwight Clark, "A Forgotten Evanston Institution: The Northwestern Female College," *Journal of the Illinois State Historical Society* 35 (June 1942): 115–32.

[14] Hale, "May Wright Sewall," Chapter 3, Page 5.

[15] Ibid., Chapter 4, Page 6.

[16] Ibid., Chapter 6, Page 13.

[17] "Edwin Walter Thompson," *Indianapolis Evening News,* 27 August 1875.

[18] George P. Brown, "Women in the Schools," in James H. Smart, ed., *The Indiana Schools and the Men Who Have Worked in Them* (Cincinnati: Wilson, Hinkle & Company, 1875), 179.

[19] Richard G. Boone, *A History of Education in Indiana* (1892; reprint, Indianapolis: Indiana Historical Bureau, 1941), 302, 318.

[20] See, Harold Littell, "Development of the City School System of Indiana—1851–1880 (Concluded)," *Indiana Magazine of History* 12 (December 1916): 309, and Elba L. Branigin, *History of Johnson County, Indiana* (Indianapolis: B. F. Bowen & Company, 1913), 270–71.

[21] See, Boone, *A History of Education in Indiana,* 218; James H. Madison,

The Indiana Way: A State History (Bloomington and Indianapolis: Indiana Historical Society and Indiana University Press, 1986), 179–80; Jacob P. Dunn Jr., *Greater Indianapolis: The History, the Industries, the Institutions, and the People of a City of Homes,* 2 vols. (Chicago: The Lewis Publishing Company, 1910), 1:275; and William J. Reese, "Urban School Reform in the Victorian Era," in William J. Reese, ed. *Hoosier Schools: Past and Present* (Bloomington: Indiana University Press, 1998), 31.

[22] Hale, "Which May Wright Sewall," Indianapolis Woman's Club Papers, IHS.

[23] Dunn, *Greater Indianapolis,* 1:271–73.

[24] See, Laura Sheerin Gaus, *Shortridge High School, 1864–1981: In Retrospect* (Indianapolis: Indiana Historical Society, 1985), 9–12; Amy C., Schutt, "Abram Crum Shortridge," in *Encyclopedia of Indianapolis,* 1259; and Dunn, *Greater Indianapolis,* 1:273–74.

[25] David Starr Jordan, *The Days of a Man: Being Memories of a Naturalist, Teacher and Minor Prophet of Democracy* (Yonkers-on-Hudson, NY: World Book Company, 1922), 129–30. See also, Gaus, *Shortridge High School,* 21.

[26] Brown, "Women in the Schools," 183. In addition to Thompson, other women teachers at Indianapolis High School mentioned by Brown were Fidelia Anderson, Emily Johnson, Mary McGregory, Rhoda Driggs, Mary Nicholson, Ellen F. Thompson (May Thompson's sister-in-law), Emma A. Greene, S. M. Lovejoy, Eliza F. Ford, and Mrs. N. A. Stone. Ibid.

[27] Helen McKay Steele, "My Indianapolis," Theodore L. Steele Papers, IHS. See also, Connie J. Zeigler, "Ovid Bulter," in *Encyclopedia of Indianapolis,* 370–71, and *Indianapolis Woman's Club, 1875–1940* (Greenfield, Ind.: William Mitchell Printing Company, 1944), 16.

[28] Martha Nicholson McKay, *Literary Clubs of Indiana* (Indianapolis: The Bowen-Merrill Company, 1894), 48. An Indiana politician claimed that the financial panic that gripped the nation in 1873 and 1874 actually aided Indiana's intellectual growth through groups like the College Corner Club. The prosperity following the Civil War were "molding the people into wealth-worshipers, and when their wealth was suddenly swept away, they turned to find the treasures which are neither to be lost nor depreciated in value.' Ibid., 16–17.

[29] Eva Draegert, "Cultural History of Indianapolis: Literature, 1875–1890," *Indiana Magazine of History* 52 (September 1956): 223–24. See also, *Indianapolis Woman's Club,* 16.

[30] Ross F. Lockridge Sr., *The Old Fauntleroy Home* (New Harmony, Ind.: New Harmony Memorial Commission, 1939), 125–26.

[31] Ibid., 126–27. See also, Jennie Cunningham Croly, *The History of the*

Woman's Club Movement in America (New York: Henry G. Allen & Company, 1898), 432.

[32] Sara M. Evans, *Born for Liberty: A History of Women in America* (New York: The Free Press, 1989), 139–40. See also, Nancy Woloch, *Women and the American Experience,* 2nd edition (New York: McGraw Hill, 1994), 289.

[33] *Indianapolis Woman's Club,* 18.

[34] McKay, *Literary Clubs of Indiana,* 43.

[35] *Indianapolis Woman's Club,* 41.

[36] Ibid., 20–24. See also, Minutes, 18 February 1875, Indianapolis Woman's Club Papers, IHS. Because the minutes at that first meeting of the Indianapolis Woman's Club did not list all those present, there has been some disagreement on which women were responsible for founding the organization. Using the group's first two meetings as a base, the club's founders are generally agreed as the following: McKay, Nicholson, Clarke, Julian, Manlove, Martin, Thompson, Katherine L. Dorsey, Henrietta Athon Morrison, Elizabeth Nicholson, Sarah R. Perrine, and Nancy G. Roberts. See, Leigh Darbee, "Focus: '—and ladies of the club': The Indianapolis Woman's Club at 125," *Traces of Indiana and Midwestern History* 12 (Spring 2000): 26–29.

[37] Constitution, Indianapolis Woman's Club, Indianapolis Woman's Club Papers, IHS. See also, Woloch, *Women and the American Experience,* 289.

[38] *Indianapolis Woman's Club,* 27.

[39] Ibid., 29–30.

[40] McKay, *Literary Clubs of Indiana,* 44.

[41] Ibid., 44–45.

[42] Indianapolis Woman's Club, 41. See also, Darbee, "Focus: '—and ladies of the club'," 29, and Draegert, "Cultural History of Indianapolis," 224.

[43] *As the Little Daughter of the President Sees the Club* (Indianapolis: Indianapolis Woman's Club, 1925), n.p.

[44] See, Woloch, *Women and the American Experience,* 289–90, and Croly, *The History of the Woman's Club Movement in America,* 13.

[45] "Obituary, Edwin Walter Thompson," *Indianapolis Evening News,* 27 August 1875.

[46] Hale, "May Wright Sewall," Chapter 8, Page 2.

[47] Ibid., Chapter 8, Page 1.

Chapter Two

[1] May Wright Sewall, "Indiana," in Elizabeth Cady Stanton, Susan B. Anthony, and Matilda Joslyn Gage, eds., *The History of Woman Suffrage*, 6 vols. (1886; reprint, Salem, N.H.: Ayer Company, 1985), 3:535–36.

[2] L. Alene Sloan, "Some Aspects of the Woman Suffrage Movement in Indiana," Ph.D. diss., 1982, Ball State University, Muncie, Ind., 77–78.

[3] *History of Woman Suffrage*, 3: 537. See also, Connie J. Zeigler, "Women's Rights and Suffrage" in Robert G. Barrows and David Bodenhamer, eds., *Encyclopedia of Indianapolis* (Bloomington: Indiana University Press, 1994), 1,445–48.

[4] Jane Stephens, "May Wright Sewall: An Indiana Reformer," *Indiana Magazine of History* 78 (December 1982): 286. See also, Helen M. Gougar, "Sketch of May Wright Sewall," *Our Herald*, 13 December 1884.

[5] Ida Husted Harper, *Life and Work of Susan B. Anthony*, 3 vols. (1898; reprint, New York: Arno and the *New York Times*, 1969), 1:510–11. In addition to Thompson, other suffragists mentioned by Harper included Zerelda Wallace, Frances Willard, Julia and Rachel Foster, Clara B. Colby, M. Louise Thomas, Laura and Sallie Clay Bennett, and Elizabeth Boynton Harbert. All these women, said Harper, became "her [Anthony's] devoted adherents and fellow-workers, and whose homes and hospitality she enjoyed during all the years which followed." Ibid., 511. See also, Judith E. Harper, *Susan B. Anthony: A Biographical Companion* (Santa Barbara, Calif.: ABC-CLIO, 1998), 178.

[6] Justin E. Walsh, *The Centennial History of the Indiana General Assembly, 1816–1978* (Indianapolis: Select Committee on the Centennial History of the Indiana General Assembly, 1987), 166.

[7] See, Sloan, "Some Aspects of the Woman Suffrage Movement," 19, and Emma Lou Thornbrough, *Indiana in the Civil War Era, 1850–1880* (1965; reprint, Indianapolis: Indiana Historical Society, 1989), 34–35.

[8] Elizabeth Cady Stanton, Susan B. Anthony, and Matilda Joslyn Gage, eds., *History of Woman Suffrage*, 6 vols. (1881; reprint, Salem, N.H.: Ayer Company, 1985), 1:298–99.

[9] Jacob Piatt Dunn Jr., *Indiana and Indianans: A History of Aboriginal and Territorial Indiana and the Century of Statehood*, 6 vols. (Chicago and New York: American Historical Society, 1919), 1:461–62. Bolton and Drake managed to secure subscriptions from more than a hundred women for the memorial to Owen and presented him with an antique silver pitcher on 28 May 1851 at the Indiana Statehouse. Owen thanked Bolton for her efforts, writing her: "I think it will always be a pleasant reflection to you that by dint of perseverance through many obstacles, you have so efficiently contributed to the good cause of the

property rights of your sex." Ibid. 463. See also, Zeigler, "Women's Rights and Suffrage," 1,445–48.

[10] Barbara Jane Stephens, "May Wright Sewall (1844–1920)," Ph.D. diss, Ball State University, May 1977, 128. See also, *History of Woman Suffrage*, 1:310.

[11] See, Record Book of the Indiana Woman Suffrage Assocation, Indiana Historical Society, Indianapolis; Sloan, "Some Aspects of the Woman Suffrage Movement," 21; and Thornbrough, *Indiana in the Civil War Era*, 36–7. For reaction to the petition from legislators and Indiana newspapers, see, Pat Creech Scholten, "A Public 'Jollification': The 1859 Women's Rights Petition before the Indiana Legislature," *Indiana Magazine of History* 72 (December 1976): 347–59.

[12] Sloan, "Some Aspects of the Woman Suffrage Movement," 37.

[13] *History of Woman Suffrage*, 3:534. See also, Sloan, "Some Aspects of the Woman Suffrage Movement," 48.

[14] See, Aileen S. Kraditor, *The Ideas of the Woman Suffrage Movement, 1890–1920* (1965; reprint, New York: W. W. Norton and Company, 1981), 3–4; Marjorie Spruill Wheeler, "A Short History of the Woman Suffrage Movement in America," in Wheeler, ed., *One Woman, One Vote: Rediscovering the Woman Suffrage Movement* (Troutdale, Ore.: NewSage Press, 1995), 9–10; and Judith E. Harper, *Susan B. Anthony: A Biographical Companion* (Santa Barbara, Calif.: ABC–CLIO, 1998), 10–12.

[15] *History of Woman Suffrage*, 3:534, 537.

[16] Inez Haynes Irwin, *Angels and Amazons: A Hundred Years of American Women* (Garden City, N.Y.: Doubldeday, Doran and Company, 1933), 229.

[17] Lucy Stone to Martha McKay, 31 July 1878, Theodore L. Steele Papers, IHS.

[18] May Wright Thompson to Martha McKay, 4 August 1878, Steele Papers, IHS.

[19] Lucy Stone to Martha McKay, 20 September 1878, Steele Papers, IHS.

[20] Lucy Stone to May Wright Thompson, 7 October 1878, and Indianapolis Equal Suffrage Society resolution dated 22 October 1878, Steele Papers, IHS.

[21] Mary Livermore to Martha McKay, 9 January 1880, Steele Papers, IHS.

[22] See, Stephens, "May Wright Sewall (1844–1920)," 11, 64–5; "Theodore L. Sewall," in *Pictorial and Biographical Memoirs of Indianapolis and Marion County, Indiana* (Chicago: Goodspeed Brothers, 1893), 321–22; "Theodore L. Sewall Dead," *Indianapolis News*, 23 December 1895; and "Theodore L. Sewall Memorial Meeting Held by the Alumnae Association and Members of the Girls' Classical School," 6 January 1896, Indiana Division, Indiana State Library, Indianapolis. Elliott had written Albert E. Fletcher of Indianapolis in April 1876

that if five gentlemen in the city "will guarantee twenty pupils at $150 a year, or even $100 a year for a Classical School proper, I have no doubt that I could recommend to you a competent teacher who will take care of himself after the first year or two. . . . I cordially sympathize with the desire of parents at the West to keep their young children at home; but the only way to keep them is to establish *good* schools at their doors." Stephens, "May Wright Sewall (1844–1920)" 65.

[23] Notice for a Classical School, 14 September 1876, Girls' Classical School Scrapbooks, Indiana Division, ISL.

[24]"Theodore L. Sewall Memorial Meeting Held by the Alumnae Association and Members of the Girls' Classical School," 6 January 1896, Indiana Division, ISL.

[25] Newspaper clipping dated 2 January 1877, Girls' Classical School Scrapbooks, Indiana Division, ISL.

[26] "Indianapolis Classical School," *Indianapolis Journal*, 11 September 1877.

[27] Grace Julian Clarke, "May Wright Sewall: In Memoriam," Grace Julian Clarke Papers, Manuscript Section, ISL.

[28] Hester Anne Hale, "May Wright Sewall: Avowed Feminist," Indiana Historical Society, Chapter 11, Page 5.

[29] Quoted in *New York World*, 16 March 1893.

[30] Clarke, "May Wright Sewall: In Memoriam," Manuscript Section, ISL.

[31] See, "Theodore L. Sewall Memorial Meeting," Indiana Division, ISL.

[32] Clarke, "May Wright Sewall: In Memoriam," Manuscript Section, ISL.

[33] Caroline Dunn, *History of the Indianapolis Propylaeum* (Indianapolis: n.p., 1938), 28–29.

[34] Alice Stone Blackwell to May Wright Sewall, 13 October 1897, May Wright Sewall Papers, Indianapolis–Marion County Public Library, Indianapolis.

[35] May Wright Sewall to Sarah Andrews Spencer, 16 January 1880, Clarke Papers, Manuscript Section, ISL.

[36] *History of Woman Suffrage*, 3:537.

[37] Charles Kettleborough, *Constitution Making in Indiana: A Source Book of Constitutional Documents with Historical Introduction and Critical Notes*, vol. 2 (1916; reprint, Indianapolis: Indiana Historical Bureau, 1975), 194.

[38] *History of Woman Suffrage*, 3:540, 552.

[39] Robert C. Kriebel, *Where the Saints Have Trod: The Life of Helen Gougar* (West Lafayette, Ind.: Purdue University Press, 1985), 84. Before the 1881 legislative sessions approximately five thousand copies of Tippecanoe County attorney DeWitt Wallace's opinion that the state legislature had the authority to determine presidential electors and "need not be limited or controlled by a

state constitution restricting the vote to white male citizens" had been printed and distributed around the state by woman's suffrage supporters. Ibid.

[40] *History of Woman Suffrage*, 3:541. See also, Jacob P. Dunn Jr., *Greater Indianapolis: The History, the Industries, the Institutions, and the People of a City of Homes* 2 vols., (Chicago: The Lewis Publishing Company, 1910), 1:456; Clifton J. Phillips, *Indiana in Transition: The Emergence of an Industrial Commonwealth, 1880–1920* (Indianapolis: Indiana Historical Bureau and Indiana Historical Society, 1968), 18, 499; Sloan, "Some Aspects of the Woman Suffrage Movement," 84; and Kettleborough, *Constitution Making in Indiana*, 2:194–95.

[41] Sloan, "Some Aspects of the Woman Suffrage Movement," 89. See also, *History of Woman Suffrage*, 3:551. Colonel W. R. Holloway, who edited the *Times*, had years earlier been editor for the *Indianapolis Journal* when that newspaper had described the first meeting of the Indiana Woman's Rights Association following the Civil War as comparing "favorably with the best that have ever been conducted by our own set. Whatever was said, was said with earnestness and for a purpose; and while several times the debate was considerably spiced, the ladies never fell below their brothers in sound sense." Ibid., 534.

[42] May Wright Sewall, "Women's Work," *Indianapolis Times*, 16 April 1882.

[43] Sewall, "Women's Work," *Indianapolis Times*, 7 January 1883. See also, Stephens, "May Wright Sewall," *IMH*, 277.

[44] *History of Woman Suffrage*, 3:541.

[45] Ibid., 3:542–3. See also, Sloan, "Some Aspects of the Woman Suffrage Movement," 95–6, and Kriebel, *Where the Saints Have Trod*, 85.

[46] Sewall, "Women's Work," 24 December 1881. See also, Hale, "May Wright Sewall," Chapter 12, Page 9.

[47] Kettleborough, *Constitution Making in Indiana*, 2:208.

[48] Ibid., 207–8. See also, Sloan, "Some Aspects of the Woman Suffrage Movement," 98, and Dunn, *Indiana and Indianans*, 2:715, 1061.

[49] *History of Woman Suffrage*, 3:543.

[50] Kriebel, *Where the Saints Have Trod*, 85–94. Even after her court victory, Gougar endured harsh words from newspapers around the state. One paper, the *New Albany Public Press*, called the Lafayette reformer "a noisy, meddlesome, disagreeable partisan politician in petticoats." Ibid., 93.

[51] *History of Woman Suffrage*, 3:543. See also, Walsh, *Centennial History of the Indiana General Assembly*, 171.

[52] William Dudley Foulke, *A Hoosier Autobiography*. (New York: Oxford University Press, 1922), 84–5. See also, Sloan, "Some Aspects of the Woman Suffrage Movement," 97–8.

[53] See, Kettleborough, *Constitution Making in Indiana*, 2:211–12; Walsh, *Centennial History of the Indiana General Assembly*, 171; and *History of Woman Suffrage*, 3:543–44.

[54] Kettleborough, *Constitution Making in Indiana*, 2:222–23.

[55] Foulke, *A Hoosier Autobiography*, 74. See also, Kettleborough, *Constitution Making in Indiana*, 232–33.

[56] *History of Woman Suffrage*, 3:544.

[57] Sewall, "Women's Work," *Indianapolis Times*, 2 March 1884.

[58] See, Susan B. Anthony and Ida Husted Harper, *History of Woman Suffrage*, 6 vols. (1902; reprint, Salem, N.H.: Ayer Company, 1985), 4:19, 36.

[59] See, Stephens, "May Wright Sewall (1844–1920)," 149–50, and *History of Woman Suffrage*, 3:544.

[60] Sloan, "Some Aspects of the Woman Suffrage Movement," 91.

[61] Phillips, *Indiana in Transition*, 499.

[62] See, Stephens, "May Wright Sewall (1844–1920)," 151, and *History of Woman Suffrage*, 616.

[63] Harper, *Life and Work of Susan B. Anthony*, 2:630–32.

[64] J. Murphy to Elbert Hubbard, 25 June 1987, Sewall Papers, I–MCPL.

[65] "Mrs. Gougar in Kansas," *Lafayette Morning Journal*, 11 September 1893. See also, Kriebel, *Where the Saints Have Trod*, 139.

[66] Kriebel, *Where the Saints Have Trod*, 139.

[67] Susan B. Anthony to May Wright Sewall, 19 August 1898, Clarke Papers, Manuscript Section, ISL.

[68] Susan B. Anthony to May Wright Sewall, 20 December 1897, Clarke Papers, Manuscript Section, ISL.

[69] Harper, *Susan B. Anthony*, 178.

Chapter Three

[1] Claude Bowers, *My Life: The Memoirs of Claude Bowers* (New York: Simon and Schuster, 1962), 14. See also, Edward A. Leary, *Indianapolis: The Story of a City* (Indianapolis: Bobbs-Merrill Company, 1971), 135–38.

[2] Mary McLaughlin Reminiscences, Manuscript Section, Indiana State Library, Indianapolis.

[3] Charlotte Cathcart, *Indianapolis from Our Old Corner* (Indianapolis: Indiana Historical Society, 1965), 23.

[4] McLaughlin Reminiscences, Manuscript Section, ISL.

[5] Ibid.

[6] May Wright Sewall, *The Domestic and Social Effects of the Higher Education*

of Women: Read before the Western Association of Collegiate Alumnae, at Ann Arbor, Mich., Dec. 10, 1887 (n.p., n.d.), 17.

[7] Alexander Urbiel, "Education, Female," in Robert G. Barrows and David Bodenhamer, eds., *Encyclopedia of Indianapolis* (Bloomington: Indiana University Press, 1994), 526–27. See also, Jacob Piatt Dunn Jr., *Greater Indianapolis: The History, the Industries, the Institutions, and the People of a City of Homes,* 2 vols. (Chicago: The Lewis Publishing Company, 1910), 1:130, and Jane Stephens, "May Wright Sewall: An Indiana Reformer," *Indiana Magazine of History* 78 (December 1982): 278–9.

[8] Catalogue for Indianapolis School for Girls, Girls' Classical School Scrapbooks, Indiana Division, ISL. See also, Stephens, "May Wright Sewall," 278–79.

[9] Cathcart, *Indianapolis from Our Old Corner,* 21.

[10] May Wright Sewall, "Women's Work," *Indianapolis Times,* 3 December 1881.

[11] F. A. Cotton, *Education in Indiana: An Outline of the Growth of the Common School System, Together with Statements Relating to the Condition of Secondary and Higher Education in the State and a Brief History of the Education Exhibit* (Indianapolis: William B. Burford, 1904), 486.

[12] See, Thomas Woody, *A History of Women's Education in the United States,* 2 vols. (New York and Lancaster, Penn.: The Science Press, 1929), 2:122, and Jane Stephens, "May Wright Sewall: An Indiana Reformer," *IMH,* 279.

[13] Indianapolis Classical School circular dated March 1881, Girls' Classical School Scrapbooks, Indiana Division, ISL.

[14] May Wright Sewall, Introduction to "Symposium on Women's Dress," *The Arena* 34 (September 1892): 490.

[15] Circular dated 3 October 1882, Girls' Classical School Scrapbooks, Indiana Division, ISL.

[16] Ibid. See also, Circular from May Wright Sewall dated 25 September 1883, Girls' Classical School Scrapbooks, Indiana Division, ISL.

[17] Girls' Classical School catalog dated 21 May 1883, Girls' Classical School Scrapbooks, Indiana Division, ISL.

[18] Newspaper clipping, Girls' Classical School Scrapbooks, Indiana Division, ISL.

[19] Undated newspaper clipping from the Indianapolis News, Girls' Classical School Scrapbooks, Indiana Division, ISL.

[20] See, Mary Waldon, "Girls Classical School Building Becoming Just A Memory," *Indianapolis Star,* 22 November 1963.

[21] Untitled biographical information on May Wright Sewall, Indianapolis

Propylaeum Papers, Indiana Historical Society, Indianapolis.

[22] Circular to parents dated 1 January 1887, Girls' Classical School Scrapbooks, Indiana Division, ISL.

[23] John Goodnow to Albert Beveridge, 7 September 1904, May Wright Sewall Papers, Indianapolis–Marion County Public Library, Indianapolis.

[24] Ida Husted Harper, *Life and Work of Susan B. Anthony*, 3 vols. (1898; reprint, New York: Arno and the New York Times, 1969), 2:650.

[25] Cathcart, *Indianapolis from Our Old Corner*, 22.

[26] See, "Mrs. May Wright Sewall's Girls Classical School," *Our Herald*, 27 September 1884.

[27] Indianapolis Classical School for Girls, special announcement, 1886–87, Girls' Classical School Scrapbooks, Indiana Division, ISL.

[28] Dunn, *Greater Indianapolis*, 1:613.

[29] Theodore L. Sewall to Noble C. Butler, 28 November 1889, Noble C. Butler Papers, IHS.

[30] Ibid.

[31] Booth Tarkington, "Introduction," in May Wright Sewall, *Neither Dead nor Sleeping* (Indianapolis: Bobbs-Merrill Company, 1920), n.p.

[32] Bertha Damaris Knobe, "Mrs. May Wright Sewall: 'Leader of 5,000,000 Women,'" *Harper's Bazaar*, 2 June 1900, 280.

[33] Otis Skinner, *Footlights and Spotlights: Recollections of My Life on the Stage* (Indianapolis: Bobbs-Merrill Company, 1924), 296.

[34] Sewall House Visitor's Register, May Wright Sewall Papers, I–MCPL.

[35] Ibid. See also, Hester Anne Hale, "May Wright Sewall: Avowed Feminist," IHS, Chapter 16, Page 5.

[36] Clifton J. Phillips, *Indiana in Transition: The Emergence of an Industrial Commonwealth, 1880–1920* (Indianapolis: Indiana Historical Bureau and Indiana Historical Society, 1968), 544–545, and Marion S. Garmel, "Visual Arts," in *Encyclopedia of Indianapolis*, 210.

[37] May Wright Sewall, "The Art Association of Indianapolis, Indiana; A Retrospect," in *Art Association of Indianapolis, Indiana: A Record, 1883–1906* (Indianapolis: Hollenbeck Press, 1906), 5–7, 10. See also, Dunn, *Greater Indianapolis*, 1:484; and Eva Draegert, "The Fine Arts in Indianapolis, 1880–1890," *Indiana Magazine of History* 50 (December 1954): 325; and Phillips, Indiana in Transition, 550.

[38] Sewall, "The Art Association of Indianapolis, Indiana," 7–8. See also, Dunn, *Greater Indianapolis*, 1:484–85, and Jeffery A. Duval, "Art Association of Indianapolis," in *Encyclopedia of Indianapolis*, 266. Dunn claimed that part of the reason for the school's failure lay with the association for dropping Ketcham

as a teacher at the end of the school's first year. She went on to successfully organize sketching tours in both America and Europe. Dunn, *Greater Indianapolis,* 1:485.

[39] See, Sewall, "The Art Association of Indianapolis, Indiana," 8–9, and Phillips, *Indiana in Transition,* 551.

[40] Julia Harrison Moore, "An Anecdote of Mrs. Sewall in Regard to the Propylaeum," in May Wright Sewall Papers, Manuscript Section, ISL. See also, Caroline Dunn, *A History of the Indianapolis Propylaeum: 1888–1938* (Indianapolis: s.n., 1938), 3–4.

[41] Margaret D. Chislett, "Historical Sketch," in *Indianapolis Propylaeum: Description of Building and Account of the Dedicatory Exercise Including Historical Sketch and President Address* (Indianapolis: Carlon and Hollenbeck Printers, 1891), 15–16, 24. See also, Dunn, *A History of the Indianapolis Propylaeum,* 4–5.

[42] Ibid., 17, 32. See also, Ann Mauger Colbert, "Propylaeum," in *Encyclopedia of Indianapolis,* 1,136–37.

[43] Dunn, *A History of the Indianapolis Propylaeum,* 7.

[44] Chislett, "Historical Sketch," 19–20.

[45] See, Dunn, *A History of the Indianapolis Propylaeum,* 8–9, and "Women's Club House," *Indianapolis News,* 8 May 1890.

[46] See, Margot Doane Griffith, "Historical Sketch, The Propylaeum Story," 14 February 1974, Indianapolis Propylaeum Papers, Indiana Historical Society Library.

[47] Chislett, "Historical Sketch," 21. In heaping praise upon May Wright Sewall, Chislett also thanked Sewall's husband, Theodore, for his "unobtrusive and most valuable help in conducting our enterprise to this happy end." Ibid.

[48] May Wright Sewall, "Address," in *Indianapolis Propylaeum,* 26, 31. See also, Dunn, *A History of the Indianapolis Propylaeum,* 15. The original Propylaeum on North Street became a victim of the wrecking ball in 1923, razed as part of the construction for the Indiana World War Memorial Plaza. The new Propylaeum, located at 1410 N. Delaware St., pays homage to its patroness by displaying a portrait of her painted by Theodore Steele and a trowel she used in helping to start the building of the original Propylaeum. See, Ann Mauger Colbert, "Propylaeum," in *Encyclopedia of Indianapolis,* 1,136–37.

[49] See, "Contemporary Club—50 Golden Years," *Indianapolis Times,* 13 February 1941; "Contemporary Club Prepares To Celebrate 75th Anniversary," Indianapolis Star, 28 November 1965; and Mary Jane Meeker, "Contemporary Club of Indianapolis," in *Encyclopedia of Indianapolis,* 474.

[50] Meredith Nicholson to May Shipp, 5 October 1893, Roberta West Nicholson Papers, Manuscript Section, ISL. Nicholson eventually rejoined the Contemporary Club, serving as the group's president from 1901 to 1902. See, *The Contemporary Club of Indianapolis: A Record of Forty-Six Years*, Indiana Division, ISL.

[51] McLaughlin Reminiscences, Manuscript Section, ISL.

[52] See, "Theodore L. Sewall Dead," *Indianapolis News*, 23 December 1895.

[53] Dunn, *Greater Indianapolis*, 1:487.

[54] "Princely Gift to Art," *Indianapolis Journal*, 18 May 1895. See also, Dunn, *Greater Indianapolis*, 487; Wilbur D. Peat, "History of the John Herron Art Institute," *Bulletin: John Herron Art Institute* 63 (October 1956): 27–28; and Duval, "Art Association of Indianapolis," in *Encyclopedia of Indianapolis*, 266.

[55] Sewall, "The Art Association of Indianapolis," 13–14.

[56] See, "Theodore L. Sewall Dead," *Indianapolis News*, 23 December 1895, and "Theodore L. Sewall Memorial Meeting Held by the Alumnae Association and Members of the Girls' Classical School," 6 January 1896, Indiana Division, ISL.

[57] Harper, *Life and Work of Susan B. Anthony*, 2:850.

[58] "Theodore L. Sewall Memorial Meeting Held by the Alumnae Association and Members of the Girls' Classical School," 6 January 1896, Indiana Division, ISL.

[59] Undated letter from May Wright Sewall, Girls' Classical School Scrapbooks, Indiana Division, ISL.

[60] 27 May 1896 letter from May Wright Sewall, Girls' Classical School Scrapbooks, Indiana Division, ISL.

[61] Skinner, *Footlights and Spotlights*, 297.

[62] Stephens, "May Wright Sewall: An Indiana Reformer," 280.

[63] See, Sewall, "The Art Association of Indianapolis," 14–21; Dunn, *Greater Indianapolis*, 1:487–88; and Duvall, "Art Association of Indianapolis," in *Encyclopedia of Indianapolis*, 266.

[64] Sewall, "The Art Association of Indianapolis," 21–22.

[65] May Wright Sewall to Susan B. Anthony, 15 September 1903, Grace Julian Clarke Papers, Manuscript Section, ISL.

[66] May Wright Sewall, "To the Friends and Patrons of the Girls' Classical School," Girls' Classical School Scrapbooks, Indiana Division, ISL. See also, Stephens, "May Wright Sewall (1844–1920)," 93, and William J. Reese, "Education," in *Encyclopedia of Indianapolis*, 76.

[67] May Wright Sewall, "To the Graduates of the Girls' Classical School," Girls' Classical School scrapbooks, Indiana Division, ISL. See also, Stephens, "May

Wright Sewall: An Indiana Reformer," 281.

[68] "Mrs. Sewall Will Retire," *Indianapolis News,* 16 March 1907.

[69] "Distributes Her Treasures," *Indianapolis News*, 27 June 1907.

[70] See, May Wright Sewall, "People That Go to Green Acre," *Indianapolis News,* 21 September 1907, and Hale, "May Wright Sewall," Chapter 28, Page 1.

Chapter Four

[1] "Mrs. Sewall, 76, Educator, Dead at St. Vincent's," *Indianapolis Star*, 23 July 1920.

[2] From "Statement Concerning the Various Activities Which Have Engaged the Attention of Mrs. May Wright Sewall Since Her Graduation From the Northwestern University Where She Took Her Second Degree in 1878," in Papers Relating to World's Congress of Representative Women, Indiana Division, Indiana State Library, Indianapolis.

[3] May Wright Sewall, *Genesis of the International Council of Women and the Story of its Growth, 1888–1893* (n.p., 1914), 10–11. See also, Jane Stephens, "May Wright Sewall: An Indiana Reformer," *Indiana Magazine of History* 78 (December 1982): 281–82.

[4] Bertha Damaris Knobe, "Mrs. May Wright Sewall: 'Leader of 5,000,000 Women,'" *Harper's Bazaar,* 2 June 1900, 278.

[5] See, Sewall, *Genesis of the International Council of Women,* 1–2; Barbara Jane Stephens, "May Wright Sewall (1844–1920)," Ph.D. diss., Ball State University, May 1977, 98–100; Susan B. Anthony and Ida Husted Harper, eds., *The History of Woman Suffrage*, 6 vols. (1902: reprint, Salem, N.H.: Ayer Company, 1985), 4:124–25; and *Women in a Changing World: The Dynamic Story of the International Council of Women since 1888* (London: Routledge & Kegan Paul, 1966), 11.

[6] *Women in a Changing World,* 11.

[7] See, Sewall, *Genesis of the International Council of Women*, 6–7; Stephens, "May Wright Sewall (1844–1920)," 101–2; and Inez Haynes Irwin, *Angels and Amazons: A Hundred Years of American Women* (Garden City, N.Y.: Doubleday, Doran and Company, 1933), 230.

[8] Ellen Carol Dubois, ed. *The Elizabeth Cady Stanton–Susan B. Anthony Reader: Correspondence, Writings, Speeches* Rev. ed. (Boston: Northeastern University Press, 1992), 176.

[9] Susan B. Anthony to Rachel Foster, 25 April 1887, in Patricia G. Holland and Ann D. Gordon, eds., *The Papers of Elizabeth Cady Stanton and Susan B. Anthony* (Wilmington, Del.: Scholarly Resources, 1991), microform.

[10] Susan B. Anthony to Rachel Foster, 12 May 1887, *The Papers of Elizabeth Cady Stanton and Susan B. Anthony*.

[11] Ida Husted Harper, *Life and Work of Susan B. Anthony,* 3 vols. (1898; reprint, New York: Arno and the New York Times, 1969), 2:634. Anthony also had to deal with a recalcitrant Stanton, who informed her friend that a trip across the ocean to attend the meeting celebrating the anniversary of Seneca Falls convention, which she had called into formation, so "filled her with dread" she decided not to come. Infuriated, Anthony wrote "a terrific letter to Mrs. Stanton; it will start every white hair on her head." Although Stanton agreed to attend the meeting, she arrived without having prepared a speech for the occasion. Once again, Anthony pressured her friend to action, shutting Stanton in a room at the Riggs House with pen and paper and permitting no one to see her until she had completed her speech. Ibid., 635–36.

[12] "International Council of Women," *Woman's Journal,* 7 January 1888.

[13] Sewall, *Genesis of the International Council of Women,* 10–11. See also, Stephens, "May Wright Sewall (1844–1920)," 104.

[14] *History of Woman Suffrage,* 4:132–33.

[15] See, Anna Garlin Spencer, *The Council Idea: A Chronicle of Its Prophets and a Tribute to May Wright Sewall, Architect of Its Form and Builder of Its Methods of Work* (New Brunswick, N.J.: J. Heidingsfeld Company, 1930), 12; Sewall, *Genesis of the International Council of Women,* 15–21; and *Women in a Changing World,* 14–15.

[16] Irwin, *Angels and Amazons,* 231. See also, Stephens, "May Wright Sewall (1844–1920)," 106–7, and Sewall, *Genesis of the International Council of Women,* 24, 37.

[17] Sewall, *Genesis of the International Council of Women,* 31–32.

[18] Ibid., 37–42.

[19] See, Jennie Cunningham Croly, *The History of the Woman's Club Movement in America* (New York: Henry G. Allen and Company, 1898), 90–93, and Stephens, "May Wright Sewall (1844–1920)," 110.

[20] See, Croly, *History of the Woman's Club Movement,* 94, 102; Stephens, "May Wright Sewall (1844–1920)," 110; and Irwin, *Angels and Amazons,* 232–33.

[21] Sewall, *Genesis of the International Council of Women,* 45–47.

[22] Ibid., 48–49. See also, Doris Weatherford, *A History of the American Suffragist Movement* (Santa Barbara, Calif.: ABC-CLIO, 1998), 161–62, and Jeanne Madeline Weimann, *The Fair Women* (Chicago: Academy Chicago, 1981), 32–33.

[23] Ibid., 51–52. See also, Weimann, *The Fair Women,* 523, and Stephens, "May Wright Sewall (1844–1920)," 115–16.

[24] Ibid., 55–57. See also, Stephens, "May Wright Sewall (1844–1920)," 116–17, and Harper, *Life and Work of Susan B. Anthony*, 2:745.

[25] Weimann, *The Fair Women*, 524–25.

[26] Ibid., 526, 529.

[27] Rachel Foster Avery to May Wright Sewall, 22 December 1892, May Wright Sewall Papers, Indianapolis–Marion County Public Library, Indianapolis.

[28] See, Sewall, *Genesis of the International Council of Women*, 60–61; Weimann, *The Fair Women*, 531; and Harper, *Life and Work of Susan B. Anthony*, 746.

[29] See, "Women Quarreling," *Philadelphia Press*, 20 May 1893; "Boycotted Mrs. Helen Gougar," *Rockland Argus*, 20 May 1893; and "Almost a Riot," *Cedar Rapids Republic*, 20 May 1893.

[30] See, *Women in a Changing World*, 17–19, and Leila J. Rupp, *Worlds of Women: The Making of an International Women's Movement* (Princeton, N.J.: Princeton University Press, 1997), 15.

[31] Knobe, "Mrs. May Wright Sewall," 279–80.

[32] Spencer, *The Council Idea*, 43–45. See also, Merle Curti, *Peace or War: The American Struggle*, 1636–1936 (Boston: J. S. Canner and Company, 1959), 116–17.

[33] See, *Women in a Changing World*, 21–22; Spencer, *The Council Idea*, 39; and Stephens, "May Wright Sewall (1844–1920)," 164.

[34] Spencer, *The Council Idea*, 40.

[35] See, Stephens, "May Wright Sewall (1844–1920)," 166–67, and *Women in a Changing World*, 24.

[36] May Wright Sewall, *Women, World War and Permanent Peace* (San Francisco: John J. Newbegin, 1915), xi–xii. See also, Stephens, "May Wright Sewall (1844–1920)," 168.

[37] Sewall, *Women, World War and Permanent Peace*, xviii–xxiii.

[38] Ibid., 164–65.

[39] Burnet Hershey, *The Odyssey of Henry Ford and the Great Peace Ship* (New York: Taplinger Publishing Company, 1967), ix.

[40] May Wright Sewall, "To My Dear Friends in Hoosierland," 16 December 1915, Telegrams, Letters and Other Documents Relating to the Ford Expedition, 1915–1916, Manuscript Section, ISL.

Chapter Five

[1] For the background on the Ford Peace Ship, see, Henry Ford, *My Life and Work* (1922; reprint, Salem, N.H.: Ayer Company, 1993), 244–45; Barbara S. Kraft, *The Peace Ship: Henry Ford's Pacifist Adventure in the First World War* (New York: Macmillan Publishing Company, 1978); Burnet Hershey, *The Odyssey of*

Henry Ford and the Great Peace Ship (New York: Taplinger Publishing Company, 1967); "Peace Crusade," in David L. Lewis, *The Public Image of Henry Ford: An American Folk Hero and His Company* (Detroit: Wayne State University Press, 1976); and "Peace Crusade," in Allan Nevins and Frank Ernest Hill, *Ford: Expansion and Challenge*, 1915–1933 (New York: Charles Scribner's Sons, 1957).

[2]Henry Ford to May Wright Sewall, 27 November 1915, Telegrams, Letters and Other Documents Relating to the Ford Expedition, 1915–1916, Manuscript Section, Indiana State Library, Indianapolis.

[3] See, Barbara Jane Stephens, "May Wright Sewall (1844–1920)," Ph.D. diss., Ball State University, May 1977, 172–73; Nevins and Hill, *Ford: Expansion and Challenge*, 26–28; and Hershey, 16–18. Although she supported Ford's cause and the idea of continuous mediation, Addams, head of the Woman's Peace Party, opposed the ship scheme and the grandiose pronouncements from Ford about getting the soldiers out of the trenches by Christmas. Even with these doubts, Addams had agreed to travel on the ship, but illness forced her to miss the trip. See, Nevins and Hill, *Ford: Expansion and Challenge*, 27–28, 34–35, and John C. Farrell, *Beloved Lady: A History of Jane Addams' Ideas on Reform and Peace* (Baltimore: The Johns Hopkins Press, 1967), 165–66.

[4] See, Hershey, *The Odyssey of Henry Ford*, 20–22; Nevins and Hill, *Ford: Expansion and Challenge*, 28–29; and Lewis, *The Public Image of Henry Ford*, 80.

[5] See, Nevins and Hill, *Expansion and Challenge*, 30, and Hershey, *The Odyssey of Henry Ford*, 32.

[6] May Wright Sewall, "To My Friends in Hoosierdom," 16 December 1915, Ford Expedition, Manuscript Section, ISL.

[7] Ibid. See also, John D. Barry, "The Character of the Ford Expedition," *San Francisco Bulletin*, 27 January 1916.

[8] Extract of talk by May Wright Sewall, 10 December 1915, Ford Expedition, Manuscript Section, ISL.

[9] See, 8 December 1915 issue of *The Argosy* in Sewall, Ford Expedition, Manuscript Section, ISL. See also, Hershey, *The Odyssey of Henry Ford*, 81–82.

[10] May Wright Sewall, "To My Friends in Hoosierdom," 16 December 1915, Ford Expedition, Manuscript Section, ISL.

[11] Roger Burlingame, *Don't Let Them Scare You: The Life and Times of Elmer Davis* (Philadelphia: J. B. Lippincott Company, 1961), 63.

[12] See, Hershey, *The Odyssey of Henry Ford*, 91, and Nevins and Hill, *Ford: Expansion and Challenge*, 43.

[13] Burlingame, *Don't Let Them Scare You*, 63.

[14] See, Hershey, *The Odyssey of Henry Ford*, 102–4; Kraft, *The Peace Ship*, 127;

and Nevins and Hill, *Ford: Expansion and Challenge*, 41–42.

[15] Sewall, "To My Friends in Hoosierdom," 22 December 1915, Ford Expedition, Manuscript Section, ISL.

[16] See, Hershey, *The Odyssey of Henry Ford*, 122; Nevins and Hill, Ford: *Expansion and Challenge*, 45–46; and Kraft, *The Peace Ship*, 156–58.

[17] Sewall, "To My Friends in Hoosierdom," 23 December 1915, Ford Expedition, Manuscript Section, ISL. See also, Hershey, *The Odyssey of Henry Ford*, 134–36.

[18] Ibid. See also, Hester Anne Hale, "May Wright Sewall: Avowed Feminist," Indiana Historical Society, Indianapolis, Chapter 34, Page 9.

[19] See, Sewall, "To My Friends in Hoosierdom," 24 December 1915, Ford Expedition, Manuscript Section, ISL; Kraft, *The Peace Ship*, 159; and Nevins and Hill, *Ford: Expansion and Challenge*, 47.

[20] Sewall, "To My Friends in Hoosierdom," 31 December 1915, Ford Expedition, Manuscript Section, ISL.

[21] Sewall, "To My Friends in Hoosierdom," 25 December 1915, Ford Expedition, Manuscript Section, ISL.

[22] See, Kraft, *The Peace Ship*, 163–65, and Nevins and Hill, *Ford: Expansion and Challenge*, 48–49.

[23] Nevins and Hill, *Ford: Expansion and Challenge*, 49.

[24] Merle Curti, *Peace or War: The American Struggle, 1636–1936* (Boston: J. S. Canner and Company, 1959), 245.

[25] Opinion of May Wright Sewall, 29 January 1916, Ford Expedition, Manuscript Section, ISL.

[26] Burlingame, *Don't Let Them Scare You*, 66.

[27] Hale, "May Wright Sewall," Chapter 35, Page 6.

[28] "May Wright Sewall Deplores War Frenzy Observed in East," *Indianapolis Star*, 8 April 1917.

[29] See, Clifton J. Phillips, *Indiana in Transition: The Emergence of an Industrial Commonwealth*, 1880–1920 (Indianapolis: Indiana Historical Bureau and Indiana Historical Society, 1968), 600–2, and Giles R. Hoyt, "Germans," in Robert M. Taylor Jr. and Connie A. McBirney, eds., *Peopling Indiana: The Ethnic Experience* (Indianapolis: Indiana Historical Society, 1996), 171–72.

[30] Ida Husted Harper to Grace Julian Clarke, 18 November 1919, Grace Julian Clarke Papers, Manuscript Section, ISL. Johnson also sculpted the seven-ton statue, "The Woman Movement," which featured busts of Susan B. Anthony, Elizabeth Cady Stanton, and Lucretia Mott. Commissioned by the National Woman's Party, the statue was given to the nation by the NWP on 15 February 1921, Anthony's birthday. Although Anthony had wanted the statue to be given

to the Library of Congress, it instead went to the U.S. Capitol. See, Edith Mayo, "Adelaide Johnson," in Barbara Sicherman and Carol Hurd Green, eds., *Notable American Women: The Modern Period, A Biographical Dictionary* (Cambridge, Mass.: The Belknap Press of Harvard University Press, 1980), 380–81.

[31] Harper to Clarke, 11 December 1919, Clarke Papers, Manuscript Section, ISL.

[32] See, Harper to Clarke, 9 January 1920 and 4 February 1920, Clarke Papers, Manuscript Section, ISL.

[33] May Wright Sewall, *Neither Dead nor Sleeping* (Indianapolis: Bobbs-Merrill Company, 1920), 10.

Chapter Six

[1] Booth Tarkington, "Introduction," in May Wright Sewall, *Neither Dead nor Sleeping* (Indianapolis: Bobbs-Merrill Company, 1920), n.p.

[2] Booth Tarkington to May Wright Sewall, 31 August 1918, May Wright Sewall Papers, Indianapolis–Marion County Public Library, Indianapolis.

[3] Anton Scherrer, "Book by Mrs. May Wright Sewall Revealing Talks with Dead Husband Caused a Sensation Back in 1920," *Indianapolis Times*, 11 April 1939.

[4] Elizabeth Morgan, "Miss May Wright Sewall Tells of Talks with Departed Mate," *Indianapolis Star*, 9 May 1920. One longtime friend of the Sewalls, David Starr Jordan, biologist and university president, wrote to May in 1910 that her contacts with the dead "belong to the phenomena of double consciousness, our own thoughts impressing themselves on our consciousness as they came from the outside, but I do not believe that any of these matters have an objective existence outside ourselves and our consciousness." David Starr Jordan to May Wright Sewall, 13 October 1910, Sewall Papers, I–MCPL.

[5] Ruth Brandon, *The Spiritualists: The Passion for the Occult in the Nineteenth and Twentieth Centuries* (New York: Alfred Knopf, 1983; Buffalo, N.Y.: Prometheus Books, 1984), 40. See also, Ann Braude, *Radical Spirits: Spiritualism and Women's Rights in Nineteenth-Century America* (Boston: Beacon Press, 1989), 4–6; Barbara Goldsmith, *Other Powers: The Age of Suffrage, Spiritualism, and the Scandalous Victoria Woodhull* (New York: Alfred Knopf, 1998), 28; Richard William Leopold, *Robert Dale Owen: A Biography* (Cambridge, Mass.: Harvard University Press, 1940), 323, 379–80.

[6] See, Anna Stockinger, "The History of Spiritualism in Indiana," *Indiana Magazine of History* 20 (September 1924): 280–87; Louis Martin Sears, "Robert Dale Owen as a Mystic," *Indiana Magazine of History* 24 (March 1928): 15–25; and Leopold, *Robert Dale Owen*, 329, 387.

[7] Leopold, *Robert Dale Owen*, 380.

[8] Braude, *Radical Spirits*, 2.

[9] Sewall, *Neither Dead nor Sleeping*, 1.

[10] Ibid., 3, 5–6.

[11] Ibid., 7–8.

[12] Ibid., 8–10.

[13] Morgan, "Miss May Wright Sewall Tells of Talks with Departed Mate."

[14] Sewall, *Neither Dead nor Sleeping*, 59–60.

[15] Ibid., 292–95.

[16]Ibid., 118–123, 127, 195–97. See also, Jane Stephens, "May Wright Sewall: An Indiana Reformer," *Indiana Magazine of History* 78 (December 1982): 294.

[17] James Woodress, *Booth Tarkington: Gentleman from Indiana* (Philadelphia: J. B. Lippincott Company, 1954), 39–40.

[18] Booth Tarkington to May Wright Sewall, 29 November 1918, Sewall Papers, I–MCPL.

[19] Tarkington to Sewall, 9 March 1919, Sewall Papers, I–MCPL. See also, Joanne Landers Henry, "Bobbs-Merrill Company," in Robert Barrows and David Bodenhamer, eds., *Encyclopedia of Indianapolis* (Bloomington: Indiana University Press, 1994), 331–32.

[20] Tarkington to Sewall, 8 May 1919, and Tarkington to Sewall, 4 June 1919, Sewall Papers, I–MCPL.

[21] Tarkington to Sewall, 29 July 1919, Sewall Papers, I–MCPL.

[22] Jack O'Bar, "A History of the Bobbs-Merrill Company, 1850–1940: With a Postlude Through the Early 1960s," Ph.D. diss., Indiana University, August 1975, 82.

[23] Tarkington to Sewall, 10 September 1919, Sewall Papers, I–MCPL.

[24] Grace Julian Clarke to May Wright Sewall, 7 July 1919, Sewall Papers, I–MCPL.

[25] May Wright Sewall to Hewitt Howland, 22 September 1919, Bobbs-Merrill Papers, Lilly Library, Indiana University, Bloomington, Indiana. A historian of the spiritualist movement noted that its popularity mushroomed during and after World War I. To the millions of families who lost loved ones in the conflict, "anything which gave some hope that these loved relatives were not lost for ever was seized upon." See, Brandon, *The Spiritualists*, 168.

[26] See, Hester Anne Hale, "May Wright Sewall: Avowed Feminist," Indiana Historical Society, Indianapolis, Chapter 36, Page 8; Morgan, "Miss May Wright Sewall Tells of Talks with Departed Mate;" and "Mrs. Sewall Dies at St. Vincent's," *Indianapolis News*, 23 July 1920.

[27] Sewall to Howland, 17 December 1919, Bobbs-Merrill Papers, Lilly Library.

[28] See, O'Bar, "A History of the Bobbs-Merrill Company," 92.

[29] Ibid. See also, "Men and Women," *Indianapolis Star*, 25 December 1910.

[30] Howland to Sewall, 7 January 1929, and 21 January 1920, Bobbs-Merrill Papers, Lilly Library.

[31] Sewall to Howland, 22 January 1929, Bobbs-Merrill Papers, Lilly Library.

[32] "Mrs. Sewall, Again Resident of City, Wishes World Peace," *Indianapolis News*, 20 January 1920.

[33] Sewall to Howland, 23 March 1920, Bobbs-Merrill Papers, Lilly Library.

[34] Ida Husted Harper to Grace Julian Clarke, 9 January 1920, Grace Julian Clarke Papers, Manuscript Section, Indiana State Library, Indianapolis.

[35] Sewall to Howland, 11 May 1920, Bobbs-Merrill Papers, Lilly Library.

[36] Howland to Sewall, 17 May 1920, Bobbs-Merrill Papers, Lilly Library.

[37] See, Promotional materials and advertisements for *Neither Dead nor Sleeping*, Bobbs-Merrill Papers, Lilly Library, and Howland to Sewall, 9 June 1920, Bobbs-Merrill Papers, Lilly Library.

[38] See, Sewall to Howland, 9 June 1920, Bobbs-Merrill Papers, Lilly Library, and Hale, "May Wright Sewall," Chapter 36, Page 10.

[39] Morgan, "Miss May Wright Sewall Tells of Talks with Departed Mate."

[40] Promotional materials for *Neither Dead nor Sleeping*, Bobbs-Merrill Papers, Lilly Library.

[41] Booth Tarkington, "Introduction," in Sewall, *Neither Dead nor Sleeping*, n.p.

[42] Elia W. Peattie, "Neither Dead nor Sleeping," *Chicago Tribune*, 10 July 1920.

[43] J. Keith Torbert, "More Psychic Books: One, Mrs. Sewall's, Proves Quite Readable," *New York Evening Post*, 3 July 1920.

[44] "Do the Dead Still Live? A Host of Writers Attack the Problem from Various Angles, Advancing Curious Bits of Evidence to Support Their Theories," *New York Times Book Review*, 4 July 1920.

[45] See, "Mrs. Sewall, 76, Educator, Dead at St. Vincent's," *Indianapolis Star*, 23 July 1920, and "Mrs. Sewall Dies at St. Vincent's," *Indianapolis News*, 23 July 1920.

[46] "Mrs. May Wright Sewall," *Indianapolis News*, 23 July 1920.

[47] Ida Husted Harper to Grace Julian Clarke, 18 December 1920, Clarke Papers, Manuscript Section, ISL.

[48] See, Dr. James Albert Woodburn, "Mrs. Sewall—Servant of Humanity," *Indianapolis Star*, 22 February 1921.

[49] "Two Candelabra Dedicated in Mrs. May Wright Sewall's Honor," *Indianapolis News*, 28 May 1923.

[50] Grace Julian Clarke, "May Wright Sewall: In Memoriam," Clarke Papers, Manuscript Section, ISL.

Select Bibliography

General References

Apps, Jerry. *One-Room Country Schools: History and Recollections from Wisconsin*. Amherst, Wis.: Amherst Press, 1996.

Art Association of Indianapolis, Indiana: A Record, 1883–1906. Indianapolis: Hollenbeck Press, 1906.

Barrows, Robert, and David Bodenhamer, eds. *Encyclopedia of Indianapolis*. Bloomington: Indiana University Press, 1994.

Boone, Richard G. *A History of Education in Indiana*. 1892. Reprint, Indianapolis: Indiana Historical Bureau, 1941.

Bowers, Claude. *My Life: The Memoirs of Claude Bowers*. New York: Simon and Schuster, 1962.

Brandon, Ruth. *The Spiritualists: The Passion for the Occult in the Nineteenth and Twentieth Centuries*. New York: Alfred Knopf, 1983; Buffalo: Prometheus Books, 1984.

Branigin, Elba L. *History of Johnson County, Indiana*. Indianapolis: B. F. Bowen and Company, 1913.

Braude, Ann. *Radical Spirits: Spiritualism and Women's Rights in Nineteenth-Century America*. Boston: Beacon Press, 1989.

Burlingame, Roger. *Don't Let Them Scare You: The Life and Times of Elmer Davis*. Philadelphia: J. B. Lippincott Company, 1961.

Cathcart, Charlotte. *Indianapolis from Our Old Corner*. Indianapolis: Indiana Historical Society, 1965.

Cotton, F. A. *Education in Indiana: An Outline of the Growth of the Common School System, Together with Statements Relating to the Condition of Secondary and Higher Education in the State and a Brief History of the Education Exhibit*. Indianapolis: William B. Burford, 1904.

Croly, Jennie Cunningham. *The History of the Woman's Club Movement in America*. New York: Henry G. Allen and Company, 1898.

Curti, Merle. *Peace or War: The American Struggle, 1636–1936*. Boston: J. S. Canner and Company, 1959.

DuBois, Ellen Carol. *The Elizabeth Cady Stanton–Susan B. Anthony Reader: Correspondence, Writings, Speeches*. Rev. ed. Boston: Northeastern University Press, 1992.

———. *Feminism and Suffrage: The Emergence of an Independent Women's Movement in America, 1848–1869*. Ithaca, N.Y.: Cornell University Press, 1978.

Dunn, Jacob Piatt Jr. *Greater Indianapolis: The History, the Industries, the Institutions, and the People of a City of Homes*. Vol. 1. Chicago: The Lewis Publishing Company, 1910.

————. *Indiana and Indianans: A History of Aboriginal and Territorial Indiana and the Century of Statehood*. Vol. 1. Chicago and New York: American Historical Society, 1919.

Evans, Sara M. *Born for Liberty: A History of Women in America*. New York: The Free Press, 1989.

Farrell, John C. *Beloved Lady: A History of Jane Addams' Ideas on Reform and Peace*. Baltimore: The Johns Hopkins Press, 1967.

Flexner, Eleanor and Ellen Fitzpatrick. *Century of Struggle: The Woman's Rights Movement in the United States*. 1959. Reprint, Cambridge, Mass.: The Belknap Press of Harvard University Press, 1996.

Ford, Henry. *My Life and Work*. 1922. Reprint, Salem, N.H.: Ayer Company, 1993.

Foulke, William Dudley. *A Hoosier Autobiography*. New York: Oxford University Press, 1922.

Gaus, Laura Sheerin. *Shortridge High School, 1864–1981: In Retrospect*. Indianapolis: Indiana Historical Society, 1985.

Goldsmith, Barbara. *Other Powers: The Age of Suffrage, Spiritualism, and the Scandalous Victoria Woodhull*. New York: Alfred Knopf, 1998.

Harper, Ida Husted. *Life and Work of Susan B. Anthony*. Vol. 2. 1898. Reprint, New York: Arno and the *New York Times*, 1969.

Harper, Judith E. *Susan B. Anthony: A Biographical Companion*. Santa Barbara, Calif.: ABC–CLIO, 1998.

Hershey, Burnet. *The Odyssey of Henry Ford and the Great Peace Ship*. New York: Taplinger Publishing Company, 1967.

Indianapolis Propylaeum: Description of Building and Account of the Dedicatory Exercise Including Historical Sketch and President Address. Indianapolis: Carlon and Hollenbeck Printers, 1891.

Indianapolis Woman's Club, 1875–1940. Greenfield, Ind.: William Mitchell Printing Company, 1944

Irwin, Inez Haynes. *Angels and Amazons: A Hundred Years of American Women*. Garden City, N.Y.: Doubleday, Doran and Company, 1933.

James, Edward T., ed. *Notable American Women, 1607–1950: A Biographical Dictionary*. Vol. 3. Cambridge, Mass.: The Belknap Press of Harvard University Press, 1971.

Jordan, David Starr. *The Days of a Man: Being Memories of a Naturalist, Teacher and Minor Prophet of Democracy*. Yonkers-on-Hudson, N.Y.: World Book Company, 1922.

Kettleborough, Charles. *Constitution Making in Indiana: A Source Book of Constitutional Documents with Historical Introduction and Critical Notes*. Vol. 2. 1916. Reprint, Indianapolis: Indiana Historical Bureau, 1975.

Kraditor, Aileen S. *The Ideas of the Woman Suffrage Movement, 1890–1920*. 1965. Reprint, New York: W. W. Norton and Company, 1981.

Kraft, Barbara S. *The Peace Ship: Henry Ford's Pacifist Adventure in the First World War*. New York: Macmillan Publishing Company, 1978.

Kriebel, Robert C. *Where the Saints Have Trod: The Life of Helen Gougar*. West Lafayette, Ind.: Purdue University Press, 1985.

Leary, Edward A. *Indianapolis: The Story of a City*. New York: Simon and Schuster, 1962.

Lewis, David L. *The Public Image of Henry Ford: An American Folk Hero and His Company*. Detroit: Wayne State University Press, 1976.

Leopold, Richard William. *Robert Dale Owen: A Biography*. Cambridge, Mass.: Harvard University Press, 1940.

Lockridge, Ross Sr. *The Old Fauntleroy Home*. New Harmony, Ind.: New Harmony Memorial Commission, 1939.

McKay, Martha Nicholson. *Literary Clubs of Indiana*. Indianapolis: The Bowen-Merrill Company, 1894.

Madison, James H. *The Indiana Way: A State History*. Indianapolis: Indiana Historical Society and Indiana University Press, 1986.

Nesbit, Robert C. and William F. Thompson. *Wisconsin: A History*. 2d ed. Madison, Wis.: The University of Wisconsin Press, 1989.

Nevins, Allan and Frank Ernest Hill. *Ford: Expansion and Challenge, 1915–1933*. New York: Charles Scribner's Sons, 1957.

Phillips, Clifton J. *Indiana in Transition: The Emergence of an Industrial Commonwealth, 1880–1920*. Indianapolis: Indiana Historical Bureau and Indiana Historical Society, 1968.

Pictorial and Biographical Memoirs of Indianapolis and Marion County, Indiana. Chicago: Goodspeed Brothers, 1893.

Reese, William J., ed. *Hoosier Schools: Past and Present*. Bloomington: Indiana University Press, 1998.

Rupp, Leila J. *Worlds of Women: The Making of an International Women's Movement*. Princeton, N.J.: Princeton University Press, 1997.

Sewall, May Wright. *Genesis of the International Council of Women and the Story of its Growth, 1888–1893*. N.p., 1914.

———. *Neither Dead nor Sleeping*. Indianapolis: Bobbs-Merrill Company, 1920.

————. *Women, World War and Permanent Peace*. San Francisco: John J. Newbergin, 1915.

Skinner, Otis. *Footlights and Spotlights: Recollections of My Life on the Stage*. Indianapolis: Bobbs-Merrill Company, 1924.

Smart, James H., ed. *The Indiana Schools and the Men Who Have Worked in Them*. Cincinnati: Wilson, Hinkle and Company, 1875.

Spencer, Anna Garlin. *The Council Idea: A Chronicle of its Prophets and a Tribute to May Wright Sewall, Architect of Its Form and Builder of Its Methods of Work*. New Brunswick, N.J.: Heidingsfeld Company, 1930.

Stanton, Elizabeth Cady, Susan B. Anthony, and Matilda Joslyn Gage, eds. *History of Woman Suffrage*. Vol. 3. 1886. Reprint, Salem, N.H.: Ayer Company, 1985.

Thornbrough, Emma Lou. *Indiana in the Civil War Era, 1850–1880*. 1965. Reprint, Indianapolis: Indiana Historical Society, 1989.

Walsh, Justin. *The Centennial History of the Indiana General Assembly, 1816–1978*. Indianapolis: Select Committee on the Centennial History of the Indiana General Assembly, 1987.

Ward, Geoffrey C., and Ken Burns. *Not for Ourselves Alone: The Story of Elizabeth Cady Stanton and Susan B. Anthony*. New York: Alfred Knopf, 1999.

Weatherford, Doris. *A History of the American Suffragist Movement*. Santa Barbara, Calif.: ABC-CLIO, 1998.

Weimann, Jeanne Madeline. *The Fair Women*. Chicago: Academy Chicago, 1981.

Wheeler, Marjorie Spruill, ed. *One Woman, One Vote: Rediscovering the Woman Suffrage Movement*. Troutdale, Ore.: NewSage Press, 1995.

Willard, Frances A., and Mary A. Livermore, eds. *A Woman of the Century: Fourteen Hundred-Seventy Biographical Sketches Accompanied by Portraits of Leading Women in All Walks of Life*. Buffalo: Charles Wells Moulton, 1893.

Woloch, Nancy. *Women and the American Experience*. 1984. Reprint, New York: McGraw-Hill, 1994.

Women in a Changing World: The Dynamic Story of the International Council of Women since 1888. London: Routledge & Kegan Paul, 1966.

Woody, Thomas. *A History of Women's Education in the United States*. Vol. 2. New York and Lancaster, Penn.: The Science Press, 1929.

Articles

Clark, Dwight. "A Forgotten Evanston Institution: The Northwestern Female College." *Journal of the Illinois State Historical Society* 35 (June 1942).

Darbee, Leigh. "Focus: '—and ladies of the club': The Indianapolis Woman's Club at 125." *Traces of Indiana and Midwestern History* 12 (spring 2000).

Draegert, Eva. "Cultural History of Indianapolis: Literature, 1875–1890." *Indiana Magazine of History* 52 (September 1956).

———. "The Fine Arts of Indianapolis, 1880–1890." *Indiana Magazine of History* 50 (December 1954).

Knobe, Bertha Damaris. "Mrs. May Wright Sewall: 'Leader of 5,000,000 Women.'" *Harper's Bazaar* (2 June 1900).

Littell, Harold. "Development of the City School System of Indiana—1851–1880 (Concluded)." *Indiana Magazine of History* 12 (December 1916).

"Our October Cover Page: Mrs. May Wright Sewall." *The Ladies Review* (October 1916).

Peat, Wilbur D. "History of the John Herron Art Institute." *Bulletin: John Herron Art Institute* 63 (October 1956).

Scholten, Pat Creech. "A Public 'Jollification': The 1859 Women's Rights Petition before the Indiana Legislature." *Indiana Magazine of History* 72 (December 1976).

Sears, Louis Martin. "Robert Dale Owen as a Mystic." *Indiana Magazine of History* 24 (March 1928).

Stephens, Jane. "May Wright Sewall: An Indiana Reformer." *Indiana Magazine of History* 78 (December 1982).

Stockinger, Anna. "The History of Spiritualism in Indiana." *Indiana Magazine of History* 20 (September 1924).

Vogelgesang, Susan. "Zerelda Wallace: Indiana's Conservative Radical." *Traces of Indiana and Midwestern History* 4 (Summer 1992).

Pamphlets, Papers, and Miscellaneous Sources

As the Little Daughter of the President Sees the Club. Indianapolis: Indianapolis Woman's Club, 1925.

Dunn, Caroline. *A History of the Indianapolis Propylaeum*. Indianapolis: n.p., 1938.

Hale, Hester Anne. "May Wright Sewall: Avowed Feminist." Indiana Historical Society, Indianapolis.

Jack O'Bar, "A History of the Bobbs-Merrill Company, 1850–1940: With a Postlude Through the Early 1960s," Ph.D. diss., Indiana University, 1975.

Sewall, May Wright. *The Domestic and Social Effects of the Higher Education of*

    Women: Read before the Western Association of Collegiate Alumnae, at Ann Arbor, Mich., Dec. 10, 1887.

Sloan, L. Alene. "Some Aspects of the Woman Suffrage Movement in Indiana." Ph.D. diss., Ball State University, 1982.

Stephens, Barbara Jane. "May Wright Sewall (1844–1920)." Ph.D. diss., Ball State University, May 1977.

"Theodore L. Sewall Memorial Meeting Held by the Alumnae Association and Members of the Girls' Classical School," 6 January 1896, Indiana Division, Indiana State Library, Indianapolis.

Manuscripts

Indiana Historical Society, Indianapolis
    Noble. C. Butler Papers
    Indianapolis Propylaeum Papers
    Indianapolis Woman's Club Papers
    Theodore L. Steele Papers

Indiana Division, Indiana State Library, Indianapolis
    Girls' Classical School Scrapbooks

Manuscript Section, Indiana State Library, Indianapolis
    Grace Julian Clarke Papers
    Mary McLaughlin Reminiscences
    Roberta West Nicholson Papers
    May Wright Sewall, Telegrams, Letters and Other Documents Relating to the Ford Expedition

Lilly Library, Indiana University, Bloomington
    Bobbs-Merrill Company Papers

Indianapolis–Marion County Public Library, Indianapolis
    May Wright Sewall Papers

APPENDIX 1

On 30 June 1888 Susan B. Anthony, National Woman Suffrage Association vice-president-at-large, and May Wright Sewall, NWSA executive committee chairman, issued an open letter to Republican presidential candidate Benjamin Harrison asking him to consider the following facts:

The first plank in the platform adopted by the Republican convention recently held in Chicago, entitled "The Purity of the Ballot," reaffirms the unswerving devotion of the Republican party to the personal rights and liberties of citizens in all the States and Territories of the Union, and especially to "the supreme and sovereign right of every lawful citizen, rich or poor, native or foreign, white or black, to cast one free ballot in public elections and to have that ballot duly counted." And again the platform says: "We hold the free and honest popular ballot, and the just and equal representation of all the people, to be the foundation of our republican government."

These declarations place the Republican party in its original attitude as the defender of the personal freedom and political liberties of all citizens of the United States. These sentiments, even the phraseology in which they are here expressed, may be found in every series of resolutions adopted by the National Woman Suffrage Association since its organization.

The advocates of woman suffrage would have been glad to see the phrase "male or female" inserted after the phrase "white or black" in the resolution above quoted, because this would be a fitting conclusion to the enumeration by antithesis of the classes into which citizens are divided. However, no enumeration of classes was necessary to explain or to enforce the declaration of the party's devotion to "the supreme and sovereign right of every lawful citizen to cast one free ballot in public elections and to have that ballot duly counted." It is the unimpeded exercise of this "supreme and sovereign right of every lawful citizen" which the women we represent demand.

That women are "lawful citizens" is undeniable, since the law recognizes them as such through the visits of the assessor and tax-gatherer; since it recognizes them as such in the police stations, the jails, the courts and the prisons. Only at the ballot-box is the lawful citizenship of women challenged! Only at the ballot-box, which is declared to be the sole safe-guard of the citizen's liberty—only there is the liberty of the female citizen denied.

But reverting to the first resolution in the Republican platform, so satisfactory in its sentiments, we beg to suggest that its value will depend solely upon its interpretation, and that its authoritative interpretation must be given by the leaders of the Republican party. Therefore to you, the chosen head of the party, we address ourselves, asking that your letter of acceptance to the nomination to the presidency of the United States be so framed as to indicate clearly your recognition of the fact that the Republican party has pledged itself to protect *every citizen* in the free exercise of "the supreme and sovereign right" to vote at public elections.

It appears to us that the application of Republican principles which we seek must be in harmony with your own inherited tendencies. One familiar with the history of the English-speaking people, during the last two and a half centuries, with their struggles for conscience, and freedom's sake, must deem it a matter of course that by this time the sense of individual responsibility has become strong even in the hearts of women; and the descendant of one who in the name of individual liberty stood with Cromwell against the "divine right of kings" and the tyranny consequent upon that obnoxious doctrine, can not be surprised to find himself appealed to by his country-women, in that same sacred name, to stand with the most enlightened portion of his party—with such men as Morton, Sumner and Lincoln—against the divine right of sex and the political tyranny involved in this doctrine, which in a republic presents such an anomaly.

APPENDIX 2

In 1905 Sewall entered into a partnership with Anna F. Weaver to run the Girls' Classical School. The following is a letter Sewall sent to friends and patrons of the school formally announcing the new arrangement and giving an overview of the institution's history and its influence:

The usual annual announcement of plans in relation to the coming school year will soon be issued. I wish, however, to precede it by a statement that I feel sure will command your interest.

You have already heard that in the future conduct of the Girls' Classical School, Miss Anna F. Weaver, a former student of the school, will be associated with me as joint and equal partner, sharing with me all of the responsibilities, financial as well as executive, and in every way having equal authority and equal responsibility. Regarding you as a sincere friend of an institution which has served you and been served by your loyal support in the past, I wish you to know that I take great pleasure in the aid which I have been able to call in the continued management of an institution which is my dearest personal interest in life. I, therefore, write you at this time, First—To ask you to share in my pleasure, and, Second—To ask for the continuance of the good word spoken in season which is so essential a factor in the success of any educational institution.

The Girls's Classical School, opened in September, 1882, has, during the past twenty-three years, stood without wavering for those educational principles by which its founder announced that it would be guided.

From the first day to date, it has been recognized that a child is a composite being, and that an education which concerns itself with only the child's mind is very inadequate. Always the child's body, mind, heart and soul have been recognized and provided for at the Girls' Classical School.

Believing that an institution, like a tree, can be judged by its fruits, I must refer you for the proofs of the soundness of our principles to the success of our application of them to our daily work, and to the influence of the school upon the lives of those who have been subjected to it. The school now has graduated two hundred and twenty-six young women. Of those to whom its diploma has been given, ninety-three have pursued their higher education in the best colleges and universities in this country. Several of these have supplemented such higher work by study at foreign universities. Of the one hundred and thirty-three remaining number of its graduates, many have continued their education at special schools, studying Bookkeeping, Stenography, Journalism, Music, Art, the Drama, Nursing, Medicine and Law. I am very proud to say that our graduates may be found pursuing the professions acquired in these institutions.

Of the graduates, ninety-four are married, and, I believe, uncommonly well married, and in the conduct of their own homes one may find the influence of their school nurture, discipline and culture.

One may not, of course, say that these interesting statistics are attributable to the school, but one may reasonably believe that the school has had its share in developing in its students a desire for usefulness. The influence which one may expect to see most clearly expressed in the lives of the graduates of the school, one may also find in young women in this and in other communities whose whole school education, although it fell short of graduation, has been obtained at the Classical, and in the more than twenty-five hundred other girls who have attended the School from one to eight years and yet left before their under-graduate work was completed.

Of the whole number of girls who have attended the Classical School in the last twenty-three years more than two thousand belong to Indianapolis families, the remaining number have come from twenty-eight different states and territories, so we feel that whatever influence our school exerts, has been carried to all parts of our country. One knows that such influence cannot be measured, weighed or counted, and yet these slight statistics increase one's perception of what it may have been. It is for this reason that I have ventured to trouble you with them.

I believe that the school may well claim that its work is characterized by "thoroughness, accuracy and sincerity", the objects professed in the first an-nouncement issued under its name; that its discipline is firm but affectionate, and that it has won the respect of people high in the educational world of our country. I have lately had the pleasure of reading a letter from Dr. David Starr Jordan, President of Leland Stanford Jr. University, from which I quote a pleasing sentence. Commending the school, and saying that he has know its work from the date of its founding, he adds: "Its three graduates who have entered Stanford have been in the first rank of Stanford University graduates, young women of character, thoroughness and originality." It is very pleasing to have disinterested testimony from such a witness to the success of the school in those features of its work which it most esteems and for which it works with most persistence.

Like the founder of the school, I have always intended that the Girls' Classical School should be put on a firm and permanent basis. I feel that the partnership effected with Miss Weaver is a definite step toward the change of a purely private enterprise into an endowed institution.

At this time I write,

First, to communicate the above;

Second, to thank you most heartily for the sympathy, the faith, and the actual patronage by which you have supported and helped to make possible my work;

My third and most urgent reason for writing you at this time is to assure you of my profound conviction that Miss Weaver's position in the school will be to it a source of every kind of strength,—intellectual, moral and financial,—and to solicit from you for us both, in the immediate present and in the future, that kind interest which an institution may expect from its former patrons and students,—that which will turn into strength, and such practical support as you may be able to give. I feel confident that any child whom you may be instrumental in sending to the Girls' Classical, will feel increasingly grateful for a decision that shall have placed her under its influence and secured for her the privileges of its tuition and associations.

APPENDIX 3

To recruit followers for her council idea, Sewall traveled to Europe to address an International Congress of Women, which met in Paris in July 1889. This was her first opportunity to outline her idea for an international woman's organization to a foreign audience. The following are some of her remarks at the Paris congress:

The organization which I have the honor to represent in this distinguished congress has a most significant title. It is called The National Council of Women of the United States. The origin of this organization is as significant as its name.

The National Council of Women of the United States is one of the immediate products of an International Council of Women, convened at Washington, the capital of our country, in March 1888.

The International council held in Washington was convened under the auspices of the National Woman Suffrage Association of the U.S., but it included representatives of all degrees of conservatism as well as of all degrees of radicalism; that was incomparably the most truly representative gathering of women ever convened in our country. The subjects which we considered were naturally as numerous and as various as were the organizations represented in it. Delegates from fifty-eight national organizations of women in our own country and from various organizations of women in England, Scotland, France, Norway, Denmark, Finland, Indiana and Canada, discussed under numerous sub-titles the general subjects of philanthropy, charities, temperance, moral reform and political rights, or such aspect of those subjects as particularly interest and affect women.

That council illustrated on a great scale, what had before a thousand times had been prved in a small way,—viz., that it is good for people independently holding different views and working along entirely different directions, to meet now and then on the broad lines of general agreement and human sympathy.

The conviction that such occasional meetings would benefit all who should participate in them grew from day to day through the fifteen sessions of the council in the minds of its participants, as it had grown in the mind of the chairman of its Organizing committee during the months of preparation. Out of that conviction arose the permanent National Council of Women of the United States, and also the initiatory steps toward forming a permanent International council.

The constitution of the National council, adopted at Washington, and the circular letter issued subsequently by its general officers . . . show that the object of the council is to bring all national organizations of women into a federation, and to provide for regular triennial meetings of such federation. In these meetings every cause or object represented by the National organizations which have joined the federation will be discussed by its advocates, and its progress will be officially reported. It will be seen that the National council itself, as such, does not espouse any one cause, advocate any *one* reform, or, indeed, give preference to any one above the others. All of the organizations confederated in it meet in it as equals, with equal representation on its official staff and on its executive board, whatever their respective numerical strength may be. Whether the significance of this will be understood by those unfamiliar with the conditions of American life I am uncertain, and, therefore, I shall undertake to explain one aspect of American social life which has so often excited the curiosity of travelers in our country.

De Tocqueville speaks with astonishment at the ease with which public meetings are convened in the United States, and of the tendency of American men to organize into bodies for the accomplishment of any desired purpose— for instance, as the building of a church, opening a school, mending a road, draining a swamp, approving or condemning an official.

The same "tendency to hold meetings and to organize," which De Tocqueville notices as characteristic of American men, has also developed in American women. This tendency in our men and in our women has probably the same origin. In a new country and in a society whose fundamental principle is equality, the individual man is inadequate to any great task. Individual weakness finds its sole remedy in combination. This is quite as true of women as of men. The earliest combinations of women in our country were formed in the name of religion. If men held meetings and organized associations *to build* new churches, women, on a smaller scale and by quieter methods did precisely the same thing to *furnish* the churches, when built, or to raise funds for educating young men to become pastors of such churches; following these combinations of women in the name of religion came others organized in the name of charity; most of the charities were connected with the churches, and to religion and charity the organized work of women was limited until some noble, self-sacrificing women formed an organization in the name of *freedom*, a name naturally dear to American women. It must be confessed that it was not their own freedom or the freedom or their sex for which these women combined, but they organized a society whose object was to deliver the African race in the United States from slavery. Not until 1848 did women in the United States begin to combine for the amelioration of their own condition. . . .

Since 1848 the work of organization among women has gone steadily forward. It received a great impetus during the war of the Rebellion, from 1861 to 1865, and from the latter date the tendency among American women to organize for the accomplishment of purposes too large to be attained by individual effort has grown to be a characteristic feature of American society. These organizations, in the large majority of instances, are in their beginning purely local, limited to a city or perhaps to a district of a city, to a village or perhaps to a country neighborhood. The local organizations of the same kind, i.e., for the same object, spread and multiply, and the aggregate themselves into county organizations; as similar organizations grow up in different counties the county societies aggregate themselves into state associations and finally state associations existing for the same purpose aggregate themselves into a national body. It is true that in some instances . . . an organization has been affected by persons of one mind and a common motive, living in different parts of our great country, and has at once assumed the dignity of a national association. This is, however, the rare exception; as a rule national organizations of women result from the union of state associations of a similar character, as the state organizations have first resulted from the union of similar county or local associations. In such local organizations of diverse names and purposes many millions of American women are now enrolled. In their hands are the missionary and charitable enterprises of the churches and the great philanthropies which are independent of the churches. By them the artistic taste and the literary culture of rural communities are nurtured, and by them the social life of cities is rescued from mere vulgar luxury, and is made to serve as an ally of the higher culture.

By them, great reforms which are destined to effect, and which do effect an amelioration of the human lot, regardless of sex, are carried forward. Conspicuous among these are some which have already arrived at international importance— such as the great temperance reform movement, with Frances E. Willard at its head—Society of the Red Cross, whose president, Clara Barton, is hardly less dear to foreign than to American hearts—and the Universal Peace Society, whose hope it is to bring all nations to settle their differences by peaceful arbitration instead of war, and with whose work the names of Lucretia Mott and Julia Ward Howe are intimately associated.

The good that is already accomplished by the organized effort of women in the United States is incalculable, and yet its beneficent results are checked and diminished by the fact that members of one organization are ignorant concerning the work of another organization; that organizations misconceive one another's objects and misunderstand one another's methods.

It has not infrequently happened that ignorance of each other's aims and methods has led to indifference, even to hostility between organizations that were *really*, though unconsciously, allies.

Thus, there was a time in the history of the temperance reform when its advocates deprecated any association with the advocates of woman's political enfranchisement, thinking the latter movement prejudicial to their own success.

Thus, the advocates of certain moral reforms and the leaders of certain charities have held aloof from the advocates of the collegiate education of women, under the erroneous impression that the higher education would harden the hearts of women and put a barrier between them and other women. Just as the advocates of temperance have learned that the advocates of woman's right, under a republic, to the ballot, were obtaining for them the only instrument by which they themselves could gain their specific ends, so the leaders of charities find that one of the first uses which women make of higher education when they have attained it is to lend it to philanthropy that she may more intelligently apply herself to relieving the condition of the poor and suffering; witness the report of the Association of Collegiate Alumnae on the sanitary construction and care of houses, and also the home established by them in one of the most destitute neighborhoods of New York City, and the number of them who have become trained nurses or physicians.

What I have said will make more intelligible what I desire to say about the National council, which I have the honor to represent. It is intended that its triennial meetings (all of which will, by the terms of its constitution, be held in Washington) shall accomplish several important results.

First: They will make an opportunity for women whose work is along different lines, to become personally acquainted with one another; and also to become acquainted with the purposes and the management of organizations, in which they have no part and form which they have hitherto held aloof.

Second: It is anticipated that out of acquaintance will spring reciprocal sympathy. Women will learn that the different lines along which they work are, however different, after all convergent, and destined to meet in that improved state of human society which all desire. It is neither expected nor desire that, as a result of this discovery, women will leave the work in which they are now engaged and attach themselves to other organizations. Temperament, taste, talents, opportunity, surroundings and circumstances will continue to control women in their selection of the line of work which they will undertake for the common good.

Third: We see that this National council will prove, or rather, that it will illustrate, the correlation of the spiritual forces of society. Is one, for instance, intent on feeding the hungry, nursing the sick and comforting the sorrowing?

Industrial education and the opening of new industries to women will largely diminish the number of the hungry and thus leave more food for the inevitable pensioners of society.

Let all opportunities for higher education be opened to women and their enlarged intelligence applied to domestic life will so improve the architecture and the sanitation of homes that the number of the sick will be decreased, and the invalids who remain can have the care of skilled nurses and trained physicians of their own sex. Let women have access to the learned professions as well as to all forms of industry and to all means of education—and though sorrow will not cease, it too, will diminish; for the most greivous sorrows result from sin, and the most common and degrading sins result from ignorance, poverty and helplessness.

Fourth: This illustration of the correlation of the spiritual forces of society cannot fail to exert a great and ultimately commanding influence upon public opinion in our country. The triennial meetings of the National council will be the feminine complement of the congress of the United States. Such meetings will focus public attention, reports of them which the press will convey to all parts of the country will instruct the public mind and they cannot fail to accelerate the progress of every movement which they represent.

Fifth: In these meetings will convene not the mere representatives of states of geographical territory, but in them will meet the representatives of great humanitarian enterprises, of spiritual aspirations, of political and social reforms, or moral and religious movements. As these meetings will not bring together the mere representatives of states and sections, but of causes and movements which have the same significance and the same beneficent effect in all states and in all sections, they cannot but result in cultivating in women and, therefore, in the whole people, that spirit of patriotism and of nationality, by which alone the unity of our great republic can be secured. . . .

APPENDIX 4

The following are from a series of lectures given by the deceased Theodore Sewall to his wife May Wright Sewall on psychic law, revealing to her how spirits could return and communicate with the living :

Spirit Return

The world has grown skeptical of immortality or holds the doctrine in such superstitious regard that any intelligent attempt to prove it is deemed blasphemous.

I shall assume that you know that good and simple souls, devout and God-fearing, have from the beginning of historic time claimed a knowledge of immortality. How has such knowledge been gained? Exactly as any knowledge of a foreign country has been gained, *viz.*: by going thither or by receiving thence intelligent guests capable of giving an accurate account of what they have witnessed and experienced.

Just as one who has been to another country has usually much to say that is of little interest, so much of little interest has been reported from the next plane of life.

It does not reduce the satisfaction of the courts, cathedrals, galleries, museums and scenery of Europe that many returned travelers tell you only of its restaurants, prisons and slums and that many of its natives who come hither have apparently been blind and deaf to the historic associations and the artistic treasures of the lands whence they have come.

If many people who claim in a trance state to have gotten a foretaste of the land that lies on the other side of death seem not much to have profited by the experience and as many mortals who claim to have returned thence bring information of small value, this no more discounts the facts of continuity of life and of the wealth of the resources of its next plane than does the ignorance of immigrants or the frivolity of summer tourists discount to the minds of intelligent Americans the existence and the resources of Europe and the Orient.

The important thing is to learn the route by which to reach Europe and the Orient that we may see and hear for ourselves. So the important thing is that we shall know the law by which one may enter and explore the life beyond the grave.

A spirit after the dissolution of the bond that confines it within the body experiences no change of essence or of character. The only changes are in its environment and in its capacity for movement and for communication. It finds itself unclothed of flesh but clothed upon with as real a body of finer texture which we may name *ether*. This word, a few years ago unknown and more lately uncomprehended, we now know names a stuff capable of analysis and description and adapted to as definite a use in the unfolding of humanity as it the physical atmosphere, some elements of which have now for centuries been known to man.

Ether is a fluid that interpenetrates the air; it is indeed that element in air which has escaped the analytical chemist; it is a compound substance whose elements are not yet discernible or tangible to mortal comprehension. It is a fine atmosphere surrounding as well as interpenetrating the atmosphere which we breathe and in which we find the elements that sustain our mortal bodies. It is the inhalation of the ether within the atmosphere by the mind within the body that keeps the mind in vital relation with its fleshy encasement.

Death is the severing of the etheric bond. Death separates the triune tenant from the body by the fact that the tenant is thus cut off from its connection with the ether within the atmosphere. The triune tenant is sometimes called spirit, sometimes soul by those who, without knowledge, believe in soul as the permanent substance of the human. It is usually called mind by those who realize the tenant only through its ability to acquire knowledge and who further believe that the mind's only source of knowledge or the sole mediums of its acquisition are the bodily senses.

The tenant thus disembodied (unhoused) finds itself to be still itself, moved by the same emotions, passions and aspiration as when incarnated. It finds every mental emotional and spiritual aptitude quickened by its release from the flesh. It soon realizes that the flesh which, while it remained on earth, was its chief instrument, was also its chief obstruction. Relieved of this impediment, that is of this body with its carnal passions, which must always be distinguished from the passions of the soul, the tenant naturally sets about the task of learning all that is learnable about its new conditions, and if it has strong ties with those who still remain on earth, it sets about the task of readjusting its relationships. This, disembodied spirits have been trying to do for countless ages, and, just as on earth, there is at least no historic age that has not produced illuminated men and women who have solved the question of the origin and the destiny of man, vaguely perhaps, but nobly still, so in the life on the other side of the grave also since death first was, the law of evolution has been working and severed souls have sought return and again and again have done so successfully; but just as with inventions and discoveries on earth, one age has sought out and another age has availed itself of discovery or applied the invention; so, here what the independent seekers found, what the gigantic inventors have made, have remained necessarily inoperative until, in fullness of time, an age should come, a day, *this* day, when in increasing numbers those who have experienced death try to return to earth.

Desire always precedes attainment. A desire must be approximately universal before an attainment can be reached by numbers of appreciable consequence.

Human affection is as subject to evolutionary law as is any other human quality. The germs of affections exist in all created beings, human and subhuman; but their de-velopment and their intensity depend upon the state of evolution reached. Only within recent centuries have human affections approximated maturity; so only within the same period have human affections, with any degree of universality, survived death and sent thoughts of longing back to earth. As the numbers feeling these longings have increased and as they have united to concentrate upon the Earth Plane, where loved ones have been left, the *Magnetic Force of Mass*, which is a law equally effective on all planes, has operated to draw the longings of survivors to the plane immediately reached through death, where ether, as an atmosphere and a life-sustaining element, takes the place of air as an atmosphere and as the life sustaining factor in mortal environment.

We have said that it is through ether's being inhaled by the mind, so to speak, that the mind is held in the body at all. After death, connection with the air, the atmosphere, is quite relinquished, because that air is used only by the mortal body, but the mind still is sustained by ether, and consequently the mind has the power to relate the pure ether in the realm which succeeds death to the ether, which exists on this plane of life only as an envelope of our atmosphere and as an interpenetrating fluid, still unrecognized by most incarnate humans, and still not analyzed by any. Thus the mind, after death, by long series of experimentations, finds itself capable of returning to the Earth Plane, so to speak, by the etheric route. On this plane we have great volumes of accumulated proof that excarnate humans for ages have, in increasing numbers, tried to find the return route to earth. Not until those left on earth were far enough developed affectionally and spiritually to respond in proportionate numbers to that longing, was the discovery, which was known to Socrates and which antedates his time, made available for the common use of humanity. . . .

At last, many simple people, investigating only for the solace of their wounded hearts, have experienced an unanticipated illumination of intellect and they know the Etheric Plane exactly as others know the existence of the Atlantic—because they have crossed it. They know the land, the realm, the plane, the condition beyond death exactly—to continue the parallel—as others know the lands that border the eastern shore of the Atlantic; because they have visited them, or because they have held close converse with those whose home is there and who are wonted to its conditions, its occupations, its views, its current thought. Just as the Atlantic, which was once only a name in human ears signifying something vast and vague, and indicating a barrier, an eternal separation, has become familiar to our youngest children, who alone, without mother or nurse, can cross it safely in any good captain's care—so ether, still to many a name given, as they suppose, by the overwrought fancy to a non-existing element, has, to other many, become not only a real but as definite a cognomen as oxygen itself, with which it is indeed most closely related. Ether, the atmosphere which the mind inhales so long as it needs to inhale anything to sustain its relation with the physical body—ether, which is the envelope and the interpenetrating vitality of the earth's atmospheric envelope—the existence of this ether as a condition of mental life on the Mortal Plane and as the body of the mind on the next plane, and hence as the medium of communication between the two spheres: This is the first lesson to be learned concerning PSYCHIC LAW.

Recognition

Recognition depends on continuous identity. In its normal state the mind is robed in ether. Its fleshly encasement is abnormal to mind, and also the being the *self* knows as *self* even while residing in the fleshly body. Therefore, death, which to the flesh body and to the earth-bound spirit is revolting and repugnant, is to the mind, as also to the Self, disrobed of flesh, only a pleasant transition. Even in its mortal encasement, the mind always knows itself to be different from the carnal instrument which it uses in the accomplishment of its earthy purposes. So soon as the mind discovers that the etheric realm to which it has gone is one in substance with that element within the earth's atmosphere on which it subsisted when in the body, and which is its own element, it knows that it can move out of the etheric realm and descend to its former home by virtue of this unity of elemental character.

The next desire of the mind, of the entity, of the ego, is to be recognized when it returns.

One of the most painful experiences of the human soul is to seek out its own, either only to find that they were not its own, that the relation was but temporary and easily dispensed with, or to find its own oblivious to its persistent presence and inaccessible to its solicitations.

Earth is sometime densely covered with visiting spirits, who can not gain admission to their former homes, who find indeed the heart of the very nearest one locked and bolted against their possible intrusion.

The etheric path makes return possible. What shall secure recognition?

If the returned spirits find that friends have grown inconstant, the particular circumstances will dictate their course. If really faithless because of inherent shallowness of feeling, then, if the returned spirit is also shallow, a sense of pique or disgust, such as under similar circumstances he would in his own mortal state have felt, is all. He returns to the Etheric Plane rather relieved than otherwise to feel quite free to forget the past, and "to seek fresh fields and pastures new." If, however, he discerns that the apparent infidelity is produced by an honest skepticism of his own continued existence, continued identity and consequent continuing affection, he is filled with pity for the pain born of ignorance and sets about trying to remove the pain by imparting new knowledge.

During the last decade hundreds of books, which the writers very honestly consider original, have been written by men and women on suggestions from returned spirit who desire to increase the knowledge of the world about the nature, the environment, the capacities and the habits of its *tenant* after the death of the mortal body. . . .

The first condition of personal, individual recognition is of course the acknow-ledgment in one way or the other of a spirit's presence.

This acknowledgement being received, the next thing is to arrest the attention of the friend still in mortal encasement long enough to make him *realize* his (*i.e.*, the returned spirit's) presence.

This is the crucial point and the difficulty lies in the different rates of speed with which thought is generated by the incarnate and the excarnate entity.

Fifty million miles per second is the rate at which disembodied thought travels, while thought embodied travels with any definite perception of what lies along its route at less than one-twentieth of this speed. Now, recognition between two people always depends on their being at the same place at the same time, and it consists in each one's being conscious that the other is there.

As it is almost invariably the excarnate spirit that is first familiar with the fact of the spirit's ability to return to earth, it is the excarnate, too, that must solve the problems of recognition. Practically this means that the excarnate spirit must retard his natural pace until it is reduced to one-twentieth of its normal speed; a feat just as difficult as it would be on the Earth Plane to devise a means of raising any given rate of speed to its twentieth power. Thus far this problem has been solved in but two ways.

One is in traveling over many times the distance to be traversed so that the excarnate soul, granted that it start at the same moment with the incarnate, may meet at the definite point fixed on by the former.

Here you must recall that the returning spirit has been endeavoring for a long time to obtain recognition. He first attempts to command it by referring to trivial personal incidents, because these are the most likely to arrest the interest of the friend whom he is trying to awaken to his presence. Often the result is exactly the opposite of what he had anticipated. As what he says is personal, it is probably trivial and is therefore repudiated with an assertion like "one would not return from the grave to talk about old clothes or a fishing excursion."

This repudiation of the most natural method of establishing one's identity arises from the vague, but utterly reasonable assumption that death has quite transformed its victims; that, having passed through that experience, one no longer retains knowledge of trifling mundane experiences. Sometimes a soul filled with the sense of the freedom that results from dropping the body seeks to tell something of its present state and occupations. These are of necessity so harmonious with his tastes while on earth that again what he says is rejected for the same reason that reference to incidents in his earthly career were unconvincing. Many people insist on supposing that death equalizes all souls; gives all similar tastes and similar conditions providing they were, while here, God-fearing and humanity-serving souls. This is as untrue as any one with a little independent reflection would see it to be absurd.

Men's bodies are much more alike than their minds; so in reality death robs men of that organ through which their resemblance was most easily established. Souls, being so dissimilar, when they commence, after getting recognition, to tell of their present state, will give very diverse testimony, and that upsets many people.

However, gaining recognition, although difficult, is not impossible; and it is most easily done, by what, prior to experience, would seem the most difficult of all methods, *viz.*: by quickening the consciousness of the friends remaining on earth. This process is very long and trying, involving great patience and painstaking, but in the end it is the most satisfactory. The returned spirit approaches his still incarnate friend, and, if possible, gets, so to speak, within the friend's atmosphere, and, once there, the visitor concentrates on the aura of his friend until the latter feels something unusual. The person approached does not understand or at first can not explain his sensations; he only perceives that he feels peculiar, and by and by he finds his thoughts dwelling on his departed friend. The returned friend is instantly conscious when he becomes the subject of reflection and he lingers near and appeals by a thousand cunning devices to his friend until the latter will say he is conscious of the visitor's presence. Usually this recognition is only grudgingly acknowledged, if at all. For example, you will hear one say, "If I did not know it to be impossible, I should think my brother was here last night."

The assumption that return is impossible of course retards recognition after the return has been accomplished.

A curious fact is that *consciousness* is hardly realized by one who is really awakened. This is due to the fact that spirit, being as independent of time as of space, moves so quickly that what, measured by time, would take an hour, perhaps two hours, to occur, has happened really in an instant.

The spirit still embodied can not catch more than *one million vibrations a minute*, while the disembodied spirit will execute or create *fifty million vibrations a second*. Hence the difference between the production of the one and the appreciation of the other is so great that a recognition actually experienced is often doubted the moment after one has been clearly conscious of it. The consciousness, in itself perfect, was for so brief a period that when past it is easier for the average mind to doubt and to deny it is for it to credit, retain and examine.

There is no magic in darkness; none in silence and none in solitude—except that under these conditions, *i.e., alone, quiet* and *in the dark*, it is easier to *concentrate*.

A spirit can walk in the light, but, clad in ether, which has many qualities of light, it can not be seen in the light. A spirit can speak in any noise, but noise, *i.e.,* loud or discordant sound, breaks the etheric current so that its voice can not be distinguished. A spirit can walk by a friend's side in a crowd; but the crowd so emphasizes itself upon the attention of one who is yet seeing through the bodily eye that the spirit can neither be seen or felt. Now, you will understand why one, in studying this subject, and investigating its phenomena, must work *alone, in subdued light* and in *silence*.

There is nothing uncanny, nothing *in any sense* unnatural about this any more than there is in the laws that govern investigation in any other field.

Even in the physical world, when we are all on the same plane, we take pains to arrange the conditions so that we can receive our friends in the way that will enable us to get and to give the most satisfaction during their visits.

One friend likes to go with us to market; another likes best to meet her friends when she and they are in elegant costumes, all aiding the radiance of a brilliant party; another likes to meet his friends in a game; another to read aloud or to be read to; still others like best to come into some retreat—a library, a study, a studio, a sewing-room, a den, where in the conditions best suited to each, each will disclose her own nature and study that of her host or hostess.

Excarnates, if refined, conservative, and retiring, like to see their friends in solitude, silence and twilight; but there are excarnate humans that visit their friends only at séances, public camps or places where crowds congregate, or in smaller but still miscellaneous assemblies.

The laws that govern individuality are much better obeyed on the Etheric than on the Physical Plane, and here the law that "like attracts like" holds good.

Communication By Vibration

Communication between spheres is made possible by the fact that ether, which is common to both the ante- and the post-mortem planes, and which is believed to be common to all spheres within the Solar System, has the quality which enables it to receive and transmit vibrations of all kinds, no matter on what plane or in what source they originate.

Vibrations depend on threads of connection. These threads are furnished by means of memory on the one side and of hope on the other, so long as memory and hope continue to affect both the spirits who have departed from earth and those that remain on it. By these sentiments souls that are physically separated by death are brought together.

Memory and hope, and all other sentiments, passions and emotions have each a material covering so very delicate that it is invisible and intangible to those still embodied in flesh. One of the first pleasant discoveries made by the departed human (who may be called soul, spirit, mind, ego, as you will) is that, although the flesh body was left on earth, he is not without a body, *i.e.*, a covering for all his faculties and functions—*i.e.*, for himself. One of the qualities of this covering of the sentiments is that, when active, it is projected in the direction of the object of its desire.

People who are reciprocally sympathetic, congenial as we say, are bound together by the sentiments we have mentioned. Those who love think of each other after death has separated them physically. Their thoughts, clothed in a substance as real as granite, but so delicate that a cobweb is *gross* by comparison, send this substance out like feelers. Such sentiments on the part of each act as magnets to the corresponding sentiments of the other; and being projected in the ether (which is the only atmosphere of the post-mortem state and also the intercellular matter and the envelope of the earth's atmosphere), and being reciprocally attractive, they find each other. A junction of this fine matter which constitutes the clothing of the affections and sentiments follows; and when this junction is affected the soul in the post-mortem sphere will know that such junction has taken place, and the joy which in consequence of this consciousness will agitate his whole being, will cause a vibration of this thread of connection which often results in a semi-consciousness and sometimes in entire consciousness on the part of the spirit still flesh embodied. Then the still embodied person will often say, "I feel as if ——— were here." "I am conscious of his presence," and he will sometimes add, "I really could almost believe I felt his touch."

Who that has lost any dearly beloved friends has not had this experience?

The mother feels as if the lost child were really once more pillowed on her bosom. The wife feels almost certain that her husband is present, trying to advise, aid and protect her. The simple fact is that the nominally dead and supposedly absent friend really *is* present.

Sometimes, probably often, perhaps usually, when people die they do depart from their accustomed places; but when they do so, it is not death that compels or causes their departure. Death makes the occasion for them to depart if there is no permanent tie between them and those from whom death physically separates them.

In cases where the death of the flesh body has not been seized upon as an opportunity to escape from uncongenial relationship, the soul, finding that it can reach its mourning loved ones by these thread-like garments of its emotions, which possess the curious qualities of expansion and contraction and of extension and withdrawal, works arduously, through these qualities, to awaken consciousness in those whom his death has bereaved.

Love is the most vital, *i.e.*, the most powerful of all the emotions, but it is not the only one that seeks to reach those still left on earth. Revenge, envy, hatred and all the evil passions have also this attenuated garment of finer matter, and souls that feel these passions are goaded by them into activity. They all seek their victims with the same result of effecting a juncture through the emotion, whatever it may be, that binds two souls together.

Each of these fine threads of connection may be charged with the whole force of the soul experiencing it; hence the strength and consequent length of any vibration will be determined by the strength of the soul producing it.

These vibrations are sometimes so delicate that their only expression, *i.e.*, their only communicated appreciable influence, is a slightly reduced temperature that may be likened to the passing of the lightest of cool soft breezes over the face or hands. Again the breeze expressing the presence may be so strong, definite and pronounced that it would not be unlike an electric shock.

The vibratory theory of the emotional connection of the two planes of being, here expounded, is comparable with and related to the vibratory theory of light, heat, motion and other qualities which either belong to physical matter or are expressed through it.

Ether, almost infinitely more delicate than the earth's atmosphere, is of course proportionally more sensitive and more fluid.

As a word uttered, even in a whisper, causes the atmosphere to vibrate and through this vibration carries the word to the ear, so a thought affects ether, causes a vibration in the etheric realm and is conveyed to the ear of the listener by a series of etheric waves which are set in motion by this vibration.

There are many degrees of acuteness in the senses of hearing and seeing on the earth, or what we may here for convenience call the *Atmospheric Plane*, and whatever degree of acuteness one may seem naturally to posses may be cultivated or diminished according to its use.

We know that much of nominal deafness is inattention arising from indifference; and we also know that a veritable impairment of the hearing may be retarded, reduced and almost defied by an alert attention and by that determined will to hear as much as possible which results in the habitual listening attitude.

If the bereaved person who suddenly feels as if the departed loved one were present, instead of denying the possibility of such a manifestation, would assume the listening attitude, the receptive condition, whatever degree of sensitiveness to etheric conditions he may possess, would be augmented, and, moreover, such thoughts, desires, anticipations would continue the vibrations originating in the etheric realm; cause new vibrations responding to the former like an echo; and consequently would create gradually through the use of these vibrations a pathway for the planned, intentional interchange of thoughts, feelings, etc., between the Etheric and the Atmospheric Planes.

Index